The New Covenant Fast

T M Leszko

Merging Streams Media

mergingstreamsmedia.com

The New Covenant Fast

Copyright © 2017 by T M Leszko

All rights reserved. No part of this book may be reproduced in any form without written permission from Merging Streams Media Inc.

www.mergingstreamsmedia.com

ISBN: 978-0-9959520-0-3 softcover book

ISBN: 978-0-9959520-1-0 electronic book

Cover Photo by Desiree Silva

www.desireephotoart.com

Unless otherwise identified all Scripture quotations in this publication are taken from:

THE HOLY BIBLE, NEW INTERNATIONAL VERSION®, NIV® Copyright © 1973, 1978, 1984 by International Bible Society. Used by permission of Zondervan Publishing House. All rights reserved worldwide.

DEDICATION

To my Lord and Savior Jesus Christ; the most faithful friend anyone could ever hope to know.

Many thanks to my family; your help in every phase of this project is greatly appreciated.

Table of Contents

Foreword

Introduction 9

Chapter 1 – From Genesis to Moses 13

Chapter 2 – From Joshua to Babylon and Back 31

Chapter 3 – The Return from Exile to Malachi 55

Chapter 4 – The Messiah Has Come 77

Chapter 5 – The Verse that Never Was 93

Chapter 6 – Fasting in the New Testament 115

Chapter 7 – The Fast that I Have Chosen 131

Chapter 8 – Walking It Out 147

Epilogue - Closing Thoughts 161

About the Author 165

Foreword

When you write a book, you usually reserve this section for someone who is respected and recognized to offer an introduction to the writer. You ride the coattails of their credibility and receive a boost from their notoriety. An added benefit from their recommendation is that it helps you reach into their audience or readership.

I have had the privilege over the past decades to know and in some cases befriend leaders who now hold great prominence in the body of Christ worldwide. I don't even have to look too far, for within my family, there is such an outstanding tradition of men and women who are leaders in the body of Christ. I originally considered asking them to write the foreword and had been offered that when the book was completed, I would be given their written support. However, I have chosen not to exercise their gracious generosity. I thought it best to raise no flag that might cause potential readers to pan the book because the recommending author may not be a part of their stream.

Whether this was the right choice or not, time will tell. I did this because of something I learned from my time serving in leadership in citywide prayer with the pastors from various denominations. I found that if I served the pastors out of a heart of love for them and show no personal bias, I could build relationships with those leaders and gain a level of trust. It seemed, the moment you raise a particular flag of the church or stream you were flowing in, your motives could or would be held as suspect. In the heart of all leadership in the body of Christ is the longing to have anyone come alongside and offer support in whatever forms it is needed. They are always pulled upon by others to give and are often the most neglected servants when their time of need arises. When you serve without an ulterior motive, the merging of those streams and leaders into a unity of purpose, it will not become a wearisome exercise.

I love the body of Christ. I am grateful to every stream that became a movement and has become as Paul called the church: "a pillar and buttress of the truth." Every denomination has brought something of value to the greater body of Christ and deserves the esteem of being found faithful to what God has invested in them. Every new wave of God deserves our support and patience to become mature in their vision and calling from the Lord. If we can serve one another from the Father's perspective, we would see the unity of the Spirit release an outpouring of the Spirit that will flow to the outermost regions of the communities we are trying to reach.

It is for this reason I offer no banner or person to recognize this work. My hope is that you, the reader, from whatever stream you flow can read this book and be ministered to by it, on its own merit. Read it with an open mind and a discerning heart to rightly divide the word of truth. It may just challenge your thinking and be a door of blessing to you from the Lord. It is my hope that this book contains more of Jesus than it does me; He truly is the only one worth promoting.

T M Leszko

Introduction

Everyone fasts. The precious time between sleep and wake is a fasting period. As you rest, your body makes essential adjustments that allow you to function. Your first meal breaks that fast and ramps up your body's metabolic processes that are required for your day. It is as though your body is a computer with an innumerable number of sensors processing the data and then making the necessary adaptations for each change of environment. It does all of this as part of the background operations with little to no awareness of its workings on our part. We are truly fearfully and wonderfully made as the psalmist wrote so long ago. This book is not about the physical health benefits of fasting. Neither is it about the various types of fasting being offered today that are extolling the latest health results you are seeking. This book is an examination of fasting and its use and instruction from the scriptures.

I have found it unusual that I would be sitting writing a book on the subject of fasting, as I had no issue at all with what I believed or was taught on the subject. To me, the topic was cut and dried, and I never carried a thought about it. I had practiced partial fasts and infrequently would do "day fasts." To be truthful, rarely over my forty years as a Christian would I engage in extended fasts. I am just being honest about this as it probably reflects the majority of those believers with careers and families who are running at full tilt whilst trying to be responsible kingdom-minded believers. We hear of the numerous calls to fast by the leaders we trust and admire and want to participate in their vision and passion for what they feel they are receiving from the Lord. So to that end, we hear and heed the call to fast in the measure that we can offer our participation as unto the Lord.

My entire paradigm of understanding regarding the subject of fasting changed in about the span of an hour. In the early hours of the morning while in that state between wakefulness and being asleep, I heard the Lord say something to me that jolted me from the mind-fog of waking up. Almost immediately, it was as if I was being downloaded with information that was unpacking in my mind and found myself contending against what I was hearing during that process. I was receiving scripture passages and thoughts that had no paradigm in my thinking and believing at that time. Fasting was neither in my thoughts nor was the subject of the slightest concern to me.

It made little sense at that time why the Lord was bringing this topic up. And so, for the next season, fasting would be the major focus of my studies. I began to search the scriptures from the lens and viewpoint I believe I had heard that morning. I then began categorizing all the passages and tested them to see if those things I had heard were true. Furthermore, I looked at the history of fasting as practiced in ancient cultures as well as the religious, holistic, and medical beliefs and knowledge of the practice. Lastly, I believe that no scripture is of private interpretation and so, I began to look for other writings from the early church fathers. I have endeavored to put this information into the framework of the New Covenant and how it relates to the believer.

Introduction

After doing this exercise of study and the compiling of the data, I put it on the shelf as I brooded over its value to the body of Christ. To me, fasting was a noble practice, which based on my knowledge I had no reason to devalue. I had wrestled for many months over the writing of this book because it would seem to fly crossways against so many leaders in the body of Christ that I love and admire. But I continuously felt the prompting from the Lord on this issue of His heart concerning fasting, so I decided to bring it forward to the body of Christ. What I failed to understand in the whole process was that the Lord desired to show His people a fast track to the release of what they were crying out to Him for.

I ask you to endure the history lesson found in the first three chapters. It will all make sense as we get to the heart of the matter. So, it is from this position and with great respect to the leadership within the body of Christ that I make this offering.

Chapter 1

From Genesis to Moses

In the Beginning

I have taken a different approach to the subject of fasting. I want to look at it from a chronological context of history covering the subject from a natural and spiritual perspective. By examining the subject in this manner, you will see the physical dynamics of the fast as part of the human experience as well as the emergence of fasting as a rite that became part of the religious experience of all major religions of the world. This will help give us context on this subject as we move into the New Covenant where Jesus gives us His address on fasting.

If we begin at the book of Genesis, we see the heart of the Father and its expression to Adam by His provision and blessing. He was placed in the Garden of God with everything that he wanted or chose to eat at his disposal. A mist came up out of the ground that kept the soil moist causing fruit trees and vegetables of every sort to grow to their optimum potential. Adam's responsibility was to simply tend this abundance that was there for his provision and enjoyment.

The fall of man brought an end to all of that. Adam and Eve were removed from the Garden of God and left to labor in the unforgiving soil. Through much toil from the sweat of their brows, they grew crops to survive. By the time Joseph came on the scene, the book of Genesis had recorded three major famines and the world had seen a catastrophic flood. One can only speculate how these events caused major environmental changes to the region. We read of plush valley regions now reduced to desert land by volcanic activity through what would be understood as the judgment of God.

The biblical lands of the Fertile Crescent are experiencing climate change on a monumental scale. Drinking water was an invaluable commodity not just for their sustenance, but for their crops as well. It is for that reason that you see throughout the book of Genesis the contention for control of the wells found by the people of the region. Finding water sources was so important, there is special mention in Genesis 36 of one of Esau's descendants named Anah who discovered the hot springs in the wilderness. Think about that for a moment. The first book of Moses comprising the most important events of the first two thousand years of mankind gives special mention to a man who finds water.

Early civilization was largely an agrarian society that depended on farming for their sustenance. Meat was a luxury for the common man and the livestock that was raised was primarily for milk and wool production, as in the case of sheep and goats. Food was the main focus and priority of every family. Thus, mealtime was of much significance and was regarded with an almost holy reverence. Today, we seem to be always on the run, and we scarf down food as a necessity of life with little to no afterthought. The ancient world regarded mealtime just as important as any religious rite. It was seen as the communing of families and peoples. To have food served as a meal was considered a great blessing; it was eaten with thankfulness to the one true God or the gods that were worshipped by the nations as described in the Bible.

When you look at this host of gods that were worshipped in the region, the most popular ones were the gods that prospered crops or affected crops positively; these were often the fertility gods. The Nile was worshipped as a god. Therefore, that which lived in or by the Nile must have also been a god in ancient Egyptian belief. The sun was worshipped as a god. The Canaanite god, Baal, was worshipped as the god of fertility and the one who controlled the weather. The scripture names numerous gods, which were worshipped in order to receive favor and blessings. None was more insidious than the worship of the god Molech, the sacrifice of animals and the fruit of the land was not enough to garner favor from this god; he required the sacrifice of children. This was the background of belief and culture of the ancient world. Sadly, even the children of Israel participated in the worship of these hideous gods as Psalm 106 reveals in the story of Israel's deliverance from their slavery in Egypt.

I once wondered how Israel could turn so quickly to an idol made by Aaron's hands. However, I learned that prior to Moses and his writings, all that Israel had to hold onto in its belief and culture was an oral history tying them to their ancestor Abraham and his worship of the God of heaven. After 400 years of living in Egypt, the children of Israel had probably adopted more of the Egyptian culture and eventually retained less and less of their own heritage. This is true even in our day and is a reality with almost any people group living in a new homeland and having a second generation grow up within it. Within this framework of belief and culture, it is clear why at this stage of civilization, we do not find fasting as a common religious practice. I have found no mention of it in the scripture to this point and could not find it as a religious practice by any of the gods that were worshipped in the region. Fasting was akin to lack and starvation, which was their sign of the loss of favor or judgment from the gods. This was the backdrop for the budding young clan of 70 persons who were called the children of Israel. They left the land of Canaan during the famine and moved to Egypt.

While fasting may not have been part of the religious rites in the early ancient world, it has always been a part of human existence. We fast from the time of our last meal of the evening until our first meal of the new day that is why the first meal of the day is obviously called breakfast; you break the fast. The ancient world observed that in times of great stress, emotional trauma or physical pain, the body would lose its appetite for food. They also noticed that their animals behaved in like manner when they were sick. This spawned a holistic thought of medicinal benefit that the Egyptians, and later the ancient Greeks held to, which was that fasting was a corrective cure for numerous health issues. It is probable to say that the Egyptians were the first to begin exporting this thought in the ancient world as the Mediterranean Sea was not just the catalyst of trade; it also served to expose that part of the world to the ideas and beliefs of its other cultures.

Genesis is the biblical book that recounts the history of man and his relationship with and to God. It records from the beginning of the creation to the death of Joseph, which occurred around 1800 BC or the year 1960 (approximate) on the Jewish calendar.

What we see throughout the book of Genesis is its recollection of major spiritual and historic events such as covenants between God and man. We also see a fast-paced overview of the rise of nations and their relationship or the lack thereof with their Creator. In addition to this, we see the Lord's interaction with man in the form of visitations by angels or the Lord Himself making veiled appearances on the earth and sharing communion meals with man.

Covenants between men were made with a sacred meal being shared before a sacrifice was offered. Abraham meets the Lord and the angels that were with Him, and they partake in a communion meal together. Lot meets angels sent by God to lead his family and him out of Sodom; they go first to his home and share a meal prepared in their honor. Melchizedek meets Abraham after the battle of the kings and comes bringing bread and wine. Jacob and Laban make a covenant of peace with each other and share a meal as part of their covenant. In the ancient world, the handling of issues as sacred as a covenant was confirmed with the sharing of a meal. Visitations with God through angels or the Lord came with a meal as a most important way to honor those who would come.

You will not find one single instance in the book of Genesis where a fast is done to honor or invoke the Lord to act. The book of Genesis ends with the death of Joseph, which puts the biblical timeline at approximately 1800 BC.

The First Recorded Fast

Over two thousand years of the biblical record have taken place with not one instance of fasting being recorded. The ancient world also follows a similar timeline with no documentation of any ancient religion practicing fasting to this point in recorded history. What we do see from the Egyptians is that fasting is something of a cure-all for sickness and disease. We also see fasting as a way of lamenting during sorrow or mourning and as the cause for the loss of appetite or want of food.

This now leads us to the period known as the Exodus when God delivers the children of Israel from the slavery of Egypt. They find themselves in the Sinai wilderness making their sojourn to the Promised Land.

Moses

The book of Deuteronomy describes the two recorded fasts of Moses in his retrospective from the ninth chapter, relating the events that were written in the book of Exodus. Moses writes:

> 7Remember this and never forget how you aroused the anger of the Lord your God in the wilderness. From the day you left Egypt until you arrived here, you have been rebellious against the Lord. 8At Horeb you aroused the Lord's wrath so that he was angry enough to destroy you. 9When I went up on the mountain to receive the tablets of stone, the tablets of the covenant that the Lord had made with you, **I stayed on the mountain forty days and forty nights; I ate no bread and drank no water.** 10The Lord gave me two stone tablets inscribed by the finger of God. On them were all the commandments the Lord proclaimed to you on the mountain out of the fire, on the day of the assembly.

11At the end of the forty days and forty nights, the Lord gave me the two stone tablets, the tablets of the covenant. 12Then the Lord told me, "Go down from here at once, because your people whom you brought out of Egypt have become corrupt. They have turned away quickly from what I commanded them and have made an idol for themselves."

13And the Lord said to me, "I have seen this people, and they are a stiff-necked people indeed! 14Let me alone, so that I may destroy them and blot out their name from under heaven. And I will make you into a nation stronger and more numerous than they."

15So I turned and went down from the mountain while it was ablaze with fire. And the two tablets of the covenant were in my hands. 16When I looked, I saw that you had sinned against the Lord your God; you had made for yourselves an idol cast in the shape of a calf. You had turned aside quickly from the way that the Lord had commanded you. 17So I took the two tablets and threw them out of my hands, breaking them to pieces before your eyes.

18Then once again I fell prostrate before the Lord for forty days and forty nights; I ate no bread and drank no water, *because of all the sin you had committed, doing what was evil in the Lord's sight and so arousing his anger.*

> *19 I feared the anger and wrath of the Lord, for he was angry enough with you to destroy you. But again the Lord listened to me* (Deuteronomy 9:7-19).

At this point, we see that the first two fasts recorded in Scripture are those that were conducted by Moses. These two fasts were held over a period of 40 days and were completed without food or water. But can these fasts be considered normal and within the capacity of any or all of humanity to achieve? The answer to that is no. In fact, it's impossible. While the human body can endure more than 40 days without food, it cannot go much beyond three days without water. One scientific report that I read speculated that if a person was not in sunlight and the external temperature did not exceed 50 degrees Fahrenheit, that person might be able to survive up to eight days without water. From this, we must conclude that the fasts of Moses were supernatural events and out of the realm of normal experience.

Consider the backdrop to these events; it's a critical moment where God has come down to Mt. Sinai offering all of Israel to be as priests before Him; they hear the audible voice of God as He delivers the commandments to them. It's not just a burning bush they are witnessing, but an entire mountain is aflame. A heavy cloud is also over the mountain with loud peals of thunder and lightning. God now speaks and delivers to all Israel in everyone's hearing — the Ten Commandments. The people, quite frankly, are terrified by the awesome presence of God. As a result, they change their minds and decline God's offer to make them a nation of priests.

They tell Moses to hear directly from God and pass on the information for them to obey. It is just after this all-encompassing experience that Moses enters the mountain to receive the commandments in stone, the instructions for the tabernacle and the details of the law. What is going on in the body of Moses in this supernatural environment? We have already concluded that it is a physical impossibility to fast without water for 40 days, so what has happened? One can only surmise that Moses' physical body was experiencing something like a suspension of all bodily functions or he was having an out of body experience as he communed with the Lord.

Furthermore, after coming down the mountain at the news that the people were worshipping a golden calf, with little to no recuperation time, he returns to go up the mountain. He must take two new hewn tablets and go again into the presence of God for another 40 days with no food or water. Under normal circumstances, his body would fail; Moses is already an old man in his eighties.

In the gospel record, we are given the events that occurred on the Mount of Transfiguration, where Moses and Elijah appear to Jesus. This time, the transfigured Jesus in all His glory is the person who illuminates the mountain as Moses and Elijah meet with Him. These two symbolize the law and the prophets and are outshone by the glory of Jesus. He would soon fulfill all the requirements of the Old Covenant and usher in the New Covenant with His royal commandment, as named by James' epistle, "to love one another."

The Law of First Mention

There is a principle that students of the scriptures and scholars alike accept as good biblical practice; it is called, the Law of First Mention. The premise of this is laid out in the following:

According to the Biblical Research Studies Group, **the Law of First Mention** is a "principle that requires one to go to that portion of the Scriptures where a doctrine is mentioned for the first time and to study the first occurrence of the same in order to get the fundamental inherent meaning of that doctrine."

What that simply means is that when you see a theme or thought from Scripture being introduced for the first time, that theme or thought will convey itself through all future references and can be understood to be literal or spiritual in its application.

So if we accept this premise of the Law of First Mention, our understanding from this first fast would lead to the following conclusion. Fasts of 40 days in Scripture signify that a supernatural encounter is in progress; this will prove to be true of every fast of 40 days that is recorded in the Bible. This will be our template to examine all other future events concerning fasts of 40 days in Scripture.

So as we close the Torah, which are the first five books of the Bible, we see that the only recorded and known fasts were conducted by Moses. But wait! How can you say this? What about Yom Kippur, otherwise known as the Day of Atonement?

Some teachers have alluded to this subject as the "God ordained" fast of the Old Covenant. So let's first look at the scriptures for insight:

The Day of Atonement

> 26The Lord said to Moses, 27"The tenth day of this seventh month is the Day of Atonement. Hold a sacred assembly and deny yourselves, and present a food offering to the Lord. 28Do not do any work on that day, because it is the Day of Atonement, when atonement is made for you before the Lord your God. 29Those who do not deny themselves on that day must be cut off from their people. 30I will destroy from among their people anyone who does any work on that day. 31You shall do no work at all. This is to be a lasting ordinance for the generations to come, wherever you live. 32It is a day of sabbath rest for you, and you must deny yourselves. From the evening of the ninth day of the month until the following evening you are to observe your sabbath" (Leviticus 23: 26-32).

> 7"On the tenth day of this seventh month hold a sacred assembly. You must deny yourselves and do no work. 8Present as an aroma pleasing to the Lord a burnt offering of one young bull, one ram and seven male lambs a year old, all without defect. 9With the bull offer a grain offering of three-tenths of an ephah of the finest flour mixed with oil; with the ram, two-tenths; 10and with each of the seven

lambs, one-tenth. 11Include one male goat as a sin offering, in addition to the sin offering for atonement and the regular burnt offering with its grain offering, and their drink offerings (Numbers 29:7-11).

The first key clarification that we must make is the differentiation of the scriptural practice of Yom Kippur from the current practice in Judaism. After the destruction of the first temple by the Babylonians and the 70 years of exile, the nation of Israel was scattered throughout the Babylonian Empire. The Jewish religious leadership had to adapt the Day of Atonement for a religion that no longer had its temple. After the destruction of the second temple by the Romans in 70 AD, the convocation days, or feast days as they had become known, had to be changed again. Modern Judaism as we see it today is markedly different in its post-temple worship than how it was practiced in the Old Testament.

The first corporate act of the Day of Atonement is described in Leviticus 16; it is the sacrificial offering for the sin of the priesthood and the nation. It was to be a completely consumed burnt offering to the Lord. Any remains and ashes were to be taken outside the camp to be disposed of. None of the meat from the sacrifice for this solemn offering was to be eaten by the priests. It is then that every individual would dedicate the day in observances according to the Law of Moses.

In the books of Leviticus and Numbers, the people were instructed that no work should be performed on this day of self-examination. They were commanded to afflict their souls and consider if there was any unconfessed sin in their lives. There has been considerable debate as to what it means to afflict the soul. However, it is clear: it does not refer to fasting in its definition and the scripture gives no instruction of a fast and how it would be conducted. I have found one version of the Bible that translates this to mean to go without food, but that is a complete liberty taken by the translators of that version. The word that is translated "to afflict" is from the Hebrew word *anah* which literally means, "to be bowed down or afflicted." This word is almost always translated as afflict, afflicted, afflicting, humble, humbling or humbled. There is no defined connective connotation to the absence of food or fasting. If an individual chooses to fast on that day as a way to afflict his or her soul, that person does so at his or her own prerogative.

Most Rabbinic scholars have concluded that the Day of Atonement was for self-examination; it was to afflict or trouble one's soul and humble one's self before the Lord. The purpose of this self-examination was for the people to carefully examine the possibilities that they might have sinned in the past year. This was different from actual, known sins that were committed throughout the year where you would immediately make a sin offering at the temple for the particular offense. No work was permitted on that day and with somber reflection, it was to be regarded as a Sabbath unto the Lord. Today, to my knowledge, only the reform branch of Judaism recognizes the Day of Atonement as a day of fasting.

What is compelling to this discussion is that Israel ate manna for forty years in the wilderness. According to Moses and Nehemiah, there is never an implied missed day of provision. There would have been at least 39 commemorations of the Day of Atonement that would have been observed during those wilderness years, with no scriptural instruction given, not to eat manna on that day. Here is what the Bible records:

> *"The people of Israel ate the manna forty years, till they came to a habitable land. They ate the manna till they came to the border of the land of Canaan. 36(An omer is the tenth part of an ephah)"* (Exodus 16:35).

> *"Because of your great compassion you did not abandon them in the wilderness. By day the pillar of cloud did not fail to guide them on their path, nor the pillar of fire by night to shine on the way they were to take. 20You gave your good Spirit to instruct them. You did not withhold your manna from their mouths, and you gave them water for their thirst"* (Nehemiah 9:19, 20).

In the gospel of John, the people bring forward the discussion of manna to Jesus. They had witnessed the feeding of the five thousand and because of this, they wanted to make Jesus a king over them. They did not care how this was to take place, even if it meant that force would be used on Jesus to make this happen. They went looking for Him and on the very next day, they found Him in Capernaum. The following exchange took place:

> *25When they found him on the other side of the lake, they asked him, "Rabbi, when did you get here?"*

> *26Jesus answered, "Very truly I tell you, you are looking for me, not because you saw the signs I performed but because you ate the loaves and had your fill. 27Do not work for food that*

spoils, but for food that endures to eternal life, which the Son of Man will give you. For on him God the Father has placed his seal of approval."

28Then they asked him, "What must we do to do the works God requires?"

29Jesus answered, "The work of God is this: to believe in the one he has sent."

30So they asked him, "What sign then will you give that we may see it and believe you? What will you do? 31Our ancestors ate the manna in the wilderness; as it is written: 'He gave them bread from heaven to eat.'"

32Jesus said to them, "Very truly I tell you, it is not Moses who has given you the bread from heaven, but it is my Father who gives you the true bread from heaven. 33For the bread of God is the bread that comes down from heaven and gives life to the world."

34"Sir," they said, "always give us this bread."

35Then Jesus declared, "I am the bread of life. Whoever comes to me will never go hungry, and whoever believes in me will never be thirsty (John 6:25-35).

This is quite the dialogue that is taking place between Jesus and the people. They want Him to be their king, but they also want proof that He is the Messiah. The evidence that they want is to be fed in the manner that the Israelites were fed under Moses. These people simply wanted their bellies filled, and they wanted Messiah to be their bakery. Jesus answers them by saying that He is the bread of heaven and what He gives will cause them to never be hungry or thirsty again. Since it is the scripture that brings forth the analogy, let's pose this question: "Will there ever be a day that you can fast Jesus out of your life with God's approval?" I think we can all agree that the answer is no. The point is we have been promised by the Lord that He will never leave us or forsake us; He will be with us always, even to the end of the world. In Christ, we are never without living water or the bread of His presence.

I'll offer one final thought before we return to the main discussion of the Day of Atonement. In the temple, the showbread or what is known as the bread of His presence was to be continually set before the Lord without exception. If God's table is always set with bread in the physical realm of the Old Covenant temple and Jesus is symbolized as our spiritual bread in the New Covenant, is His heart for His people's daily bread, anything less?

After the destruction of the first temple, the Jewish leadership in order to reflect the changes of their exile in Babylon altered the practice of the Day of Atonement. They burned incense, instead of a sacrificial burnt offering. As outlined in the Talmud, which is the oral tradition and interpretive books concerning the Law, they enacted five new regulations that were put in place for its observance. They wrote that in absence of a temple, five afflictions are required:

1. No food or water during the 25-hour period.
2. No wearing of leather shoes.
3. No anointing oneself with oil.
4. No bathing.
5. No marital relations.

Make no mistake concerning the Talmud; this is not scripture. Jesus called these and others rules adopted by the religious leaders of Israel "as the traditions of men."

The result of this study of the first five Books of Moses, otherwise known as the Torah, leads us to the following conclusion:

There is no mention of fasting apart from the obvious supernatural fasts experienced by Moses. Further to that, there was no institution of fasting as a scriptural observance under the Law of Moses. Fasting would be introduced as a rite during Israel's Babylonian captivity some 700 years later. Adding to my surprise concerning these things was that as I began my search through historical and religious works of other ancient religions running on a similar parallel timeline, there seems to be no connection to fasting for religious practice in the early stages of the ancient world? I can only present the link to the previous thoughts that I laid out earlier in this chapter as the reason for fasting at that time. It is only much later in history that fasting became associated with religious practice throughout the ancient world. The lack of food and provision was thought to be a judgment from God or the gods and not an action or practice that would incur a blessing.

The type of fasting that was practiced in the early ancient world was the result of a human holistic approach to healing the body by the physicians of that era. They deemed that fasting somehow aided the body's defenses even during the sleep process and was a type of reset button to fight the effects of illness and disease. The fact that the loss of appetite (fasting) was associated with the grieving process, also somehow connected fasting to the emotional healing process.

The New Covenant Fast

It is said that Moses died in the Jewish calendar year 2360 or approximately 1400 BC. More than one-third of the Jewish calendar's history has transpired with no fasts being enacted by God for the nation of Israel. In the next chapter, we will examine the emergence of fasting for religious purposes throughout the ancient world.

Chapter 2

From Joshua to Babylon and Back

10When you have eaten and are satisfied, praise the Lord your God for the good land he has given you. 11Be careful that you do not forget the Lord your God, failing to observe his commands, his laws and his decrees that I am giving you this day. 12Otherwise, when you eat and are satisfied, when you build fine houses and settle down, 13and when your herds and flocks grow large and your silver and gold increase and all you have is multiplied, 14then your heart will become proud and you will forget the Lord your God, who brought you out of Egypt, out of the land of slavery. 15He led you through the vast and dreadful wilderness, that thirsty and waterless land, with its venomous snakes and scorpions. He brought you water out of hard rock. 16He gave you manna to eat in the wilderness, something your ancestors had never known, to humble and test you so that in the end it might go well with you. 17You may say to yourself, "My power and the strength of my hands have produced this wealth for me." 18But remember the Lord your God, for it is he who gives you the ability to produce wealth, and so confirms his covenant, which he swore to your ancestors, as it is today. Deuteronomy 8:10-18

From the Period of the Judges and Kings to Exile in Babylon

During this early period in the times of Judges and Kings, we see in the scripture the emergence of fasting as part of the national culture of Israel. But is it really becoming a part of the religious fabric of society? In the world around them, there is little record about fasting and religion during this early period. If it was being conducted as a rite, the historical record was lost. The agricultural breakthroughs from the advent of the plow, irrigation, and seeding, and their progressive development through this period, make the founding of cities with large population bases possible. Nomadic tribal clans still exist in some areas and remain powerful, but advances in farming have made large settled people groups sustainable. This is an important development to note because the reliance on God or the pagan fertility gods for their sustenance and daily provision is not deemed as crucial to their regional survival.

Advances in shipbuilding, make the movement of goods on the Mediterranean Sea affordable and the trading coastal cities grow in prosperity and stature. As we move through this chapter, we will track and identify some of the changes by the regional nations in regard to fasting as we follow the biblical timeline. After Israel has begun to settle in the Promised Land, we start to see the first shift towards fasting. As we move forward through the scriptures, we read in the latter part of the Book of Judges, the events that led to that first recorded fast.

The First Recorded Corporate Fast

After driving out the nations through war, Israel has been dwelling in their Promised Land, for over 20 years. The first recorded fast in scripture concerning Israel as a people is not mentioned until the time of the "Judges," which takes place about 2385 on the Jewish calendar or 1375 BC. It is a period that differentiated Israel from all her surrounding neighbors because the Jewish nation was without a king. A further 330 years would elapse before Saul would be anointed its first king.

This early period would be noted in Scripture as a time when *"There was no king in Israel: every man did that which was right in his own eyes" (Judges 21:25)*. Israel could not free itself from its fascination with the pagan gods of the region. The people were already moving away from the God of their fathers in less than a generation after Joshua's death. Now, a terrible tragedy has occurred that causes the first civil war to take place between the nation and one of its tribes. Israel was to declare war with the tribe of Benjamin over a horrific event that fractured the nation. The eleven tribes consulted the Lord over the great sin of gang rape and murder committed by the Benjamites against the wife of one of Israel's priests.

The tribe of Benjamin was unwilling to cooperate with the demand for justice against the sin of the townspeople of Gibeah, and the two sides were now heading for war. The Ark of the Covenant was nearby at Bethel and the priesthood was consulted as to what should be done. They received the word of the Lord condoning the act of war and moved out with Judah leading the 10 other tribes into battle. They confidently marched out to face the Benjamites with an army of 400,000 men, armed and ready for war. On the first day of battle, a lesser force of only 26,000 men routed the army of Israel. After two days of battle, the losses to Israel were counted at 40,000 men killed and many wounded; this was more than the entire army of Benjamin. The scripture then records their response after the battle on the second day.

> *26Then all the Israelites, the whole army, went up to Bethel, and there they sat weeping before the Lord. They fasted that day until evening and presented burnt offerings and fellowship offerings to the Lord. 27And the Israelites inquired of the Lord. (In those days the ark of the covenant of God was there, 28with Phinehas son of Eleazar, the son of Aaron, ministering before it.) They asked, "Shall we go up again to fight against the Benjamites, our fellow Israelites, or not?"*
>
> *The Lord responded, "Go, for tomorrow I will give them into your hands"*
>
> (Judges 20:26-28).

Israel's eleven tribes were shattered by the devastating losses to its army. This military catastrophe with the massive loss of life caused a great cry of mourning that initiated a corporate fast by the army of Israel. They went back to Bethel, presented their offerings to the Lord, and inquired of God. Using the principle called the "Law of First Mention" again, we can establish the heartbeat or intended purpose for all corporate fasts in future texts. It suggests that the primary scriptural purpose for fasting is that of humility — to humble oneself before God.

Corporate grief for the loss of one-tenth of its warriors forced Israel to inquire of the Lord for a second time. They had sought the Lord before going to war but now, they were inquiring of Him if they should even continue to fight. In light of the context of this chapter, it is clear that fasting is a posture of humility and lowering oneself before God to inquire of Him. Their overconfidence in the fact that they had 10 times the strength of their opponents had been all but melted away after two straight days of defeat. The third day of battle turned to Israel's favor and the result of this conflict was the near obliteration of the tribe of Benjamin.

Humility before the Lord should be the position of the heart of anyone who enters a fast. Yet, as obvious as this is shown in this chapter, it will not be the case with later generations. In the future, fasting will be used as an attempt to create an obligation upon God and to manipulate Him to act on behalf of the people who are doing the fasting.

Corporate Fasts

From the death of Moses in approximately 1400 BC (2360 Jewish calendar) until the fall of Jerusalem and Judah's exile to Babylon in 585 BC (3175 Jewish calendar), a period of 800 years will have transpired. What was surprising to this study was that there were very few fasts made by Israel to call upon the Lord. When you consider the numerous wars, the breaking apart of the nation, and Israel's downward spiral into idolatry, it would seem realistic to assume that during periods of reformation within the nation, there would be numerous calls for national fasting and prayer. However, this will not prove to be the case. In fact, we will see that during this period, there are only 5 fasts recorded in Scripture. Moreover, in reality, only 3 can really even be described as "a fast unto the Lord."

Samuel Leads Israel's Reformation

Leading up to the second recorded fast in Scripture, we find that the Ark of the Covenant had been captured after Israel's defeat in its ongoing war with the Philistines. The Ark was moved to Ashdod and was kept in the temple of the pagan god Dagon. It was later returned to Israel to appease the God of Israel and end the plagues that were ravaging their country. The Ark was placed on an oxcart with some offerings of gold and immediately, the oxen left in the direction of Israel. It came to Kiriath Jearim. From this backdrop, Israel would respond to Samuel's leadership and return to the Lord. The nation would gather as one people at Mizpah and humble themselves before God with fasting and prayer. Under Samuel's prophetic leadership, the people sought the Lord and would continue to do so until Saul is anointed their first king.

> 1So the men of Kiriath Jearim came and took up the ark of the Lord. They brought it to Abinadab's house on the hill and consecrated Eleazar his son to guard the ark of the Lord. 2The ark remained at Kiriath Jearim a long time—twenty years in all.
>
> Then all the people of Israel turned back to the Lord. 3So Samuel said to all the Israelites, "If you are returning to the Lord with all your hearts, then rid yourselves of the foreign gods and the Ashtoreths and commit yourselves to the Lord and serve him only, and he will deliver you out of the hand of the Philistines." 4So the Israelites put away their Baals and Ashtoreths,

> *and served the Lord only.*
>
> *5Then Samuel said, "Assemble all Israel at Mizpah, and I will intercede with the Lord for you." 6When they had assembled at Mizpah, they drew water and poured it out before the Lord. On that day they fasted and there they confessed, "We have sinned against the Lord." Now Samuel was serving as leader of Israel at Mizpah* (1 Samuel 7:1-6).

Saul Demands a Fast of His Army While in Battle

King Saul initiated a second military fast during the ongoing wars with the Philistines. This foolhardy, copycat fast was probably based on the results of that first fast by the army of Israel. Saul recklessly demands under the threat of death that no one in the army will eat any food during the day until he has avenged his enemies. This almost cost Saul's son Jonathan his life and brought his army to the point of exhaustion and a far lesser victory.

> *24And the men of Israel had been hard pressed that day, so Saul had laid an oath on the people, saying, "Cursed be the man who eats food until it is evening and I am avenged on my enemies." So none of the people had tasted food. 25Now when all the people came to the forest, behold, there was honey on the ground. 26And when the people entered the forest, behold, the honey was dropping, but no one put his hand to his mouth, for the people feared the oath. 27But Jonathan had not heard his father charge the people with the oath, so he put out the tip of the staff that was in his hand and*

> dipped it in the honeycomb and put his hand to his mouth, and his eyes became bright. 28Then one of the people said, "Your father strictly charged the people with an oath, saying, 'Cursed be the man who eats food this day.'" And the people were faint. 29Then Jonathan said, "My father has troubled the land. See how my eyes have become bright because I tasted a little of this honey. 30How much better if the people had eaten freely today of the spoil of their enemies that they found. For now the defeat among the Philistines has not been great" (1 Sam. 14:24-30).

The army of Israel refused to let Saul exact his oath against his own son and the rout of the Philistines was left incomplete. This hardly can be considered a fast unto the Lord.

King Ahab and Queen Jezebel Proclaim a Fast in Israel

The next corporate fast in Israel is not done unto God at all, but unto the pagan god Baal. You will remember that during the rule of King Ahab and Queen Jezebel, the nation moved into almost total idolatry. Elijah thought that he was the only one left who served the God of Israel, but God had answered him that there were still seven thousand in the land who had not bowed their knees to Baal. It has been estimated that the world population in 875 BC was about 45-50 million people. Israel's population was estimated to be in excess of 2 million during the time of Ahab's rule. Some one hundred years earlier, 2 Samuel 24:9 records:

"**9** Joab reported the number of the fighting men to the king: In Israel there were eight hundred thousand able-bodied men who could handle a sword, and in Judah five hundred thousand."

This census of the armies of Israel and Judah was taken during David's reign and gives credibility that the population number is in line with the time period. Think about that for a moment, there are only 7,000 followers of the God of Israel amongst more than two million people. It is sobering to consider what Israel had become during this time, and it is from this snapshot of history, that we read the scriptural record:

> 1Some time later there was an incident involving a vineyard belonging to Naboth the Jezreelite. The vineyard was in Jezreel, close to the palace of Ahab king of Samaria. 2Ahab said to Naboth, "Let me have your vineyard to use for a vegetable garden, since it is close to my palace. In exchange I will give you a better vineyard or, if you prefer, I will pay you whatever it is worth."
>
> 3But Naboth replied, "The Lord forbid that I should give you the inheritance of my ancestors."
>
> 4So Ahab went home, sullen and angry because Naboth the Jezreelite had said, "I will not give you the inheritance of my ancestors." He lay on his bed sulking and refused to eat.
>
> 5His wife Jezebel came in and asked him, "Why

are you so sullen? Why won't you eat?" 6He answered her, "Because I said to Naboth the Jezreelite, 'Sell me your vineyard; or if you prefer, I will give you another vineyard in its place.' But he said, 'I will not give you my vineyard.' 7Jezebel his wife said, "Is this how you act as king over Israel? Get up and eat! Cheer up. I'll get you the vineyard of Naboth the Jezreelite."

8So she wrote letters in Ahab's name, placed his seal on them, and sent them to the elders and nobles who lived in Naboth's city with him. 9In those letters she wrote:

"Proclaim a day of fasting and seat Naboth in a prominent place among the people. 10But seat two scoundrels opposite him and have them bring charges that he has cursed both God and the king. Then take him out and stone him to death" (1 Kings 21:1-10).

Up to this point, I had difficulty finding surviving documentation of religious fasts during this time period. This passage reveals that fasting was a part of the rite of worship unto the pagan gods of this region. I was surprised that this historical record was found here in the book of 1 Kings. Jezebel had introduced the nation to the worship of Asherah and Baal; Israel has succumbed to this abominable idolatry. In Ahab's sulking fast, he and Jezebel will conspire and plot the murder of Naboth. When Jezebel orchestrates a fast, it is not unto the God of Israel, but unto the gods she worships.

Also worth noting is that the call to fast does not appear to have surprised anyone; it leads me to believe that these calls to fast were quite common. Naboth will be framed and murdered during the sham fast, all because the king coveted his vineyard. It was deflating to my theology that five corporate fasts were all I could find during this period and two of them were a reproach to God. This leads us to the last corporate fast that is recorded in scripture before Judah's exile to Babylon. This is what a picture of a fast unto the Lord should look like, and it takes place under Jehoshaphat's reign.

Jehoshaphat Proclaims a Day of Fasting and Prayer

> 1After this, the Moabites and Ammonites with some of the Meunites came to wage war against Jehoshaphat.
>
> 2Some people came and told Jehoshaphat, "A vast army is coming against you from Edom, from the other side of the Dead Sea. It is already in Hazezon Tamar" (that is, En Gedi). 3Alarmed, Jehoshaphat resolved to inquire of the Lord, and he proclaimed a fast for all Judah. 4The people of Judah came together to seek help from the Lord; indeed, they came from every town in Judah to seek him.
>
> 5Then Jehoshaphat stood up in the assembly of Judah and Jerusalem at the temple of the Lord in the front of the new courtyard 6and said:
>
> "Lord, the God of our ancestors, are you not the God who is in heaven? You rule over all the kingdoms of the nations. Power and might are in your hand, and no one can withstand you. 7Our God, did you not drive out the inhabitants of this land before your people Israel and give

it forever to the descendants of Abraham your friend? 8They have lived in it and have built in it a sanctuary for your Name, saying, 9'If calamity comes upon us, whether the sword of judgment, or plague or famine, we will stand in your presence before this temple that bears your Name and will cry out to you in our distress, and you will hear us and save us.'

10"But now here are men from Ammon, Moab and Mount Seir, whose territory you would not allow Israel to invade when they came from Egypt; so they turned away from them and did not destroy them. 11See how they are repaying us by coming to drive us out of the possession you gave us as an inheritance. 12Our God, will you not judge them? For we have no power to face this vast army that is attacking us. We do not know what to do, but our eyes are on you."

13All the men of Judah, with their wives and children and little ones, stood there before the Lord.

14Then the Spirit of the Lord came on Jahaziel son of Zechariah, the son of Benaiah, the son of Jeiel, the son of Mattaniah, a Levite and descendant of Asaph, as he stood in the assembly.

15He said: "Listen, King Jehoshaphat and all who live in Judah and Jerusalem! This is what the Lord says to you: 'Do not be afraid or discouraged because of this vast army. For the battle is not yours, but God's. 16Tomorrow

> march down against them. They will be climbing up by the Pass of Ziz, and you will find them at the end of the gorge in the Desert of Jeruel. 17You will not have to fight this battle. Take up your positions; stand firm and see the deliverance the Lord will give you, Judah and Jerusalem. Do not be afraid; do not be discouraged. Go out to face them tomorrow, and the Lord will be with you.'"
>
> 18Jehoshaphat bowed down with his face to the ground, and all the people of Judah and Jerusalem fell down in worship before the Lord. 19Then some Levites from the Kohathites and Korahites stood up and praised the Lord, the God of Israel, with a very loud voice (2 Chronicles 20:1-19).

The time period is around 850 BC or the year 2910, which means more than half of the Jewish calendar has elapsed. Israel and Judah have long since separated into two kingdoms: the North with its ten tribes under Ahab's rule and the tribes of Judah and Benjamin to the south under the rule of Jehoshaphat. The armies of Moab, Ammon, and Mount Seir have arrayed themselves for war against Judah. It is from this dire circumstance that the king of Judah gathers the nation together in fasting and prayer to ask the Lord for guidance as to what they should do. It is a shining moment of a people in an era where both kingdoms have had great difficulty staying faithful to the God of Israel. This act of humility will not go unnoticed or unanswered by God. The word of the Lord comes to them with a most powerful declaration that said, "The battle is the Lord's." Just as God fought the Egyptians and delivered Israel from bondage and slavery, He would again fight for His people; they will not need to raise their swords. Three armies are brought into confusion and in the fog of war begin fighting one another. The self-slaughter of these three nations was so great that it took the people of Judah three days to collect all of the spoil. This wonderful victory and awesome display of God's power still was not enough to bring forth a heart change. Israel's return to the Lord would not continue beyond Jehoshaphat's reign.

> *31So Jehoshaphat reigned over Judah. He was thirty-five years old when he became king of Judah, and he reigned in Jerusalem twenty-five years. His mother's name was Azubah daughter of Shilhi. 32He followed the ways of his father Asa and did not stray from them; he did what was right in the eyes of the Lord. 33The high places, however, were not removed, and the people still had not set their hearts on the God of their ancestors* (2 Chronicles 20:31-33).

I know this fast represents the heart and vision of every leader in the body of Christ when they proclaim a corporate fast. Their motivation comes out of humility and their hearts' cry to see a move of God come to their churches, their cities or their nations. I offer my prayer with yours, "Father, may your people see this kind of demonstration of your power come to pass from the fast that you have chosen."

The Ninevites Repent After Believing the Prophecy of Jonah

The prophet Jonah and the recounting of the City of Nineveh's repentance is the only non-Jewish corporate fast recorded in Scripture during this period. This pagan Assyrian city, estimated to have a population base of over 120,000 persons turned from their wickedness in response to Jonah's prophecy. They will fast covering themselves in sackcloth and ashes as a sign of humility to the God of Israel. This sincere act towards God will spare the city from the prophesied judgment of God.

3Jonah obeyed the word of the Lord and went to Nineveh. Now Nineveh was a very large city; it took three days to go through it. 4Jonah began by going a day's journey into the city, proclaiming, "Forty more days and Nineveh will be overthrown." 5The Ninevites believed God. A fast was proclaimed, and all of them, from the greatest to the least, put on sackcloth.

6When Jonah's warning reached the king of Nineveh, he rose from his throne, took off his royal robes, covered himself with sackcloth and sat down in the dust. 7This is the proclamation he issued in Nineveh:

"By the decree of the king and his nobles:

Do not let people or animals, herds or flocks, taste anything; do not let them eat or drink. 8But let people and animals be covered with sackcloth. Let everyone call urgently on God. Let them give up their evil ways and their violence. 9Who knows? God may yet relent and with compassion turn from his fierce anger so that we will not perish."

10When God saw what they did and how they turned from their evil ways, he relented and

> did not bring on them the destruction he had
> threatened (Jonah 3:3-10).

Individual Fasts

There are numerous fasts of a personal nature that are recorded during this period. All are out of anguish, mourning or a calamity of one kind or another – some noble and some not. From kings to the common man or woman, fasting will occur because of a loss of appetite, personal crisis or as a last ditch effort to move God to act on their behalf. We will not see the practice of fasting as a spiritual discipline or religious rite during this period. The Pharisees who fasted twice a week have not yet emerged as a sect of Judaism although they will come to prominence during the exile period. Here is a sampling of the personal fasts that we see during this period that are worth noting.

Hannah

Hannah was inconsolable and would not eat as she went before the Lord concerning her barrenness. She was tired of the continual mocking that came from her husband's other wife. She cried out to the Lord vowing to consecrate the child to Him. God answered that prayer and Samuel, the great prophet and judge in Israel was born.

David

David fasted as he mourned the deaths of Saul and Jonathan who both died in battle. He did the same for Abner, the great general of Israel, at the news of his death. We also read the very sad account of the sickness and death of his first child with Bathsheba; David fasted during the child's illness.

And the Lord afflicted the child that Uriah's wife bore to David, and he became sick. 16David therefore sought God on behalf of the child. And David fasted and went in and lay all night on the ground. 17And the elders of his house stood beside him, to raise him from the ground, but he would not, nor did he eat food with them. 18On the seventh day the child died. And the servants of David were afraid to tell him that the child was dead, for they said, "Behold, while the child was yet alive, we spoke to him, and he did not listen to us. How then can we say to him the child is dead? He may do himself some harm." 19But when David saw that his servants were whispering together, David understood that the child was dead. And David said to his servants, "Is the child dead?" They said, "He is dead." 20Then David arose from the earth and washed and anointed himself and changed his clothes. And he went into the house of the Lord and worshiped. He then went to his own house. And when he asked, they set food before him, and he ate. 21Then his servants said to him, "What is this thing that you have done? You fasted and wept for the child while he was alive; but when the child died, you arose and ate food." 22He said, "While the child was still alive, I fasted and wept, for I said, 'Who knows whether the Lord will be gracious to me, that the child may live?' 23But now he is dead. Why should I fast? Can I bring him back again? I shall go to him, but he will not return to me" (2 Sam. 12:15-23).

Elijah

Elijah has just experienced a great victory over the priests of Baal and proved to Israel that God is the Lord, not the idols they worshiped. Overcome with fear because of the death threats leveled at him by Jezebel, he flees into the wilderness feeling quite sorry for himself and is all alone.

> 1Now Ahab told Jezebel everything Elijah had done and how he had killed all the prophets with the sword. 2So Jezebel sent a messenger to Elijah to say, "May the gods deal with me, be it ever so severely, if by this time tomorrow I do not make your life like that of one of them."
>
> 3Elijah was afraid and ran for his life. When he came to Beersheba in Judah, he left his servant there, 4while he himself went a day's journey into the wilderness. He came to a broom bush, sat down under it and prayed that he might die. "I have had enough, Lord," he said. "Take my life; I am no better than my ancestors." 5Then he lay down under the bush and fell asleep.
>
> All at once an angel touched him and said, "Get up and eat." 6He looked around, and there by his head was some bread baked over hot coals, and a jar of water. He ate and drank and then lay down again.
>
> 7The angel of the Lord came back a second time and touched him and said, "Get up and eat, for the journey is too much for you." 8So he got up and ate and drank. Strengthened by

that food, he traveled forty days and forty nights until he reached Horeb, the mountain of God (1 Kings 19:1-8).

There is much spiritual allegory in this unusual 40-day fast of Elijah. As discussed earlier concerning the Law of First Mention, it was concluded that any 40-day fast in Scripture represents a supernatural event. Elijah's fast gives the opposite result of what a normal fast would do to the body. Here he is, hiding out in the wilderness in fear for his life and feeling quite sorry for himself. It's clear he isn't eating and wants to die. But our wonderful God sends an angel to him with freshly baked bread over hot coals and fresh cool water in a jar. The angel then wakes Elijah up and feeds him twice during that night. Then he sends him off on a 40-day journey covering some two hundred miles to Mount Horeb. It will be at that place that the Lord has arranged to meet with him and prepare him for his next assignment. We cannot help but to draw the analogy of Jesus who stated that He is the Bread of Life and the source of Living Water; He is our strength for the journey.

> *"Then Jesus declared, 'I am the bread of life. Whoever comes to me will never go hungry, and whoever believes in me will never be thirsty"* (John 6:35).

All spiritual hunger and thirst are satisfied in Jesus. For it is by His strength and His sustenance that we are enabled. Elijah, on the strength of those two meals, is now supernaturally enabled to travel 40 days and nights to have an encounter with God at Mt. Horeb. So, one might ask the question, "Is this passage about the fast or the meals?" I would think that in this case, the two are tied together.

Ahab

Ahab the wicked king of Israel fasts at the prophetic rebuke and judgment delivered to him through Elijah. He mourns, fasts, and covers himself in sackcloth and ashes in a real contrition of heart. Because of his humility, God responds to him:

> 27When Ahab heard these words, he tore his clothes, put on sackcloth and fasted. He lay in sackcloth and went around meekly.
>
> 28Then the word of the Lord came to Elijah the Tishbite: 29"Have you noticed how Ahab has humbled himself before me? Because he has humbled himself, I will not bring this disaster in his day, but I will bring it on his house in the days of his son" (1 Kings 21:28, 29).

Fasting among the Gentile Nations

As reported earlier, fasting is the medicinal treatment and the cure-all for almost everything in the ancient world — for both man and livestock. What we begin to see during this period is the emergence of fasting as a religious rite throughout the Fertile Crescent. The Babylonians, who have fasts commemorating their numerous gods, may have, in fact, been the chief exporters of this rite throughout the ancient world. Their Empire spanned from Egypt to the Indus Valley and they exported their religion and culture to all of their conquered foes. Their practice of deporting conquered peoples throughout the empire was meant to weaken or eradicate these other cultures as they assimilate into the Babylonian way of life. They are now on the move defeating every nation that tries to stand against them; they are now laying siege to Israel and Judah.

The Prophet Joel Proclaims a Call to Repentance

I have placed this prophetic word from the book of Joel as the last call to the people of Judah to return to the Lord. There is no record of a corresponding response by the people to this word, so I will have to assume it was not heeded. It will no longer be unusual to see prophets or kings calling out to the nation to fast and prayer. There has been some debate as to the timeline of this prophetic word, but I believe it was during the siege by the Babylonians, prior to the fall of Jerusalem and the final stage of deporting the nation to Babylon.

Despite the prophetic calls from Jeremiah and Ezekiel to return to the Lord, the southern kingdom of Judah rebels against Babylon who had defeated them in an earlier conflict. Judah has tried to make an alliance with Egypt and other nations for its defense that were contrary to the words of the Lord that were given. Instead of heeding Jeremiah's dire warnings, he would be imprisoned for his prophecies. What could appear to be the final scene before this great and sorrowful calamity are the words of the prophet Joel crying out to the nation on behalf of God.

> 13Put on sackcloth, you priests, and mourn; wail, you who minister before the altar. Come, spend the night in sackcloth, you who minister before my God; for the grain offerings and drink offerings are withheld from the house of your God. 14Declare a holy fast; call a sacred assembly. Summon the elders and all who live in the land

> to the house of the Lord your God, and cry out to the Lord. 15Alas for that day! For the day of the Lord is near; it will come like destruction from the Almighty (Joel 1:13-15).

In spite of the prophet's description of what is upon them and what will soon take place, it's as if the Lord makes one final appeal to His people.

> 12"Even now," declares the Lord, "return to me with all your heart, with fasting and weeping and mourning." 13Rend your heart and not your garments. Return to the Lord your God, for he is gracious and compassionate, slow to anger and abounding in love, and he relents from sending calamity. 14Who knows? He may turn and relent

> and leave behind a blessing—grain offerings and drink offerings for the Lord your God. 15Blow the trumpet in Zion, declare a holy fast, call a sacred assembly. 16Gather the people, consecrate the assembly; bring together the elders, gather the children, those nursing at the breast. Let the bridegroom leave his room and the bride her chamber.

> 17Let the priests, who minister before the Lord, weep between the portico and the altar. Let them say, "Spare your people, Lord. Do not make your inheritance an object of scorn, a byword among the nations. Why should they say among the peoples,

> 'Where is their God?'" (Joel 2:12-17).

Joel closes his prophecy with an offering of hope for a coming day that will signal that God is once again with His people. The apostle Peter will quote from this prophecy to declare that the Day of Pentecost is that great day of the Lord. Babylon has crushed all of the nations of the region including Egypt. All that will remain in the land of Judah will be a small poor peasant population. The walls of Jerusalem are broken down and the temple is destroyed. An exiled people will have to regroup and struggle to retain their national identity. This has all transpired by the year 586 BC or 3174 on the Jewish calendar timeline.

Chapter 3

The Return from Exile to Malachi

The Exile to Babylon

Few passages express the grief and sorrow of a people as is revealed in Psalms 137:

> 1By the rivers of Babylon we sat and wept
>
> when we remembered Zion.
>
> 2There on the poplars
>
> we hung our harps,
>
> 3for there our captors asked us for songs,
>
> our tormentors demanded songs of joy;
>
> they said, "Sing us one of the songs of Zion!"
>
> 4How can we sing the songs of the Lord
>
> while in a foreign land?
>
> 5If I forget you, Jerusalem,
>
> may my right hand forget its skill.

The New Covenant Fast

> 6May my tongue cling to the roof of my mouth
>
> if I do not remember you,
>
> if I do not consider Jerusalem
>
> my highest joy.

If there were ever a reason to grieve with fasting and prayer for the nation, this would be it. Israel and Judah have come to destruction with the loss of its two nations. But, maybe, more importantly to the souls of its people, is the destruction of their temple. They have lost the focal point of their religion. How can they deal with the issue of sin when there is no longer a temple to offer sacrifices? The northern kingdom of Israel went into captivity in 722 BC causing a flood of refugees to pour into the southern kingdom of Judah as well as the other surrounding nations. What is left of the northern kingdom and its mixed population will be the future creation of a region known as Samaria and a people known as the Samaritans. The danger to the remnant of Israel and Judah is that they might suffer the same fate in the South.

The surviving religious leadership must now from these ashes, forge a new form of their religion. In the Law of Moses, the temple was the focal point of worship and practice. They would now have to rely on the oral traditions of the law (The Mishnah) and write out the new traditions that would make up the new additions of written interpretations of the Law, which is known as the Talmud. Two diverse religious sects will emerge through this period, and they will be known as the Pharisees and Sadducees. They will vie for prominence and the doctrinal beliefs of the people.

Meanwhile, the Babylonians, after their initial invasion and victory over Judah in about 607 BC had taken the elite of Judah and Israel's brain trust and sent them to Babylon for reeducation and indoctrination. Daniel will find himself in this first wave of exiles and rise to prominence within that nation. He and the first wave of exiles will have spent about twenty years in Babylon before the remaining exiles will make their way into captivity, so it is for that reason we will start with him.

The Prophet Daniel

The book of Daniel opens with Israel's elite young men being placed in what would be something like a 3-year university education program. They are assigned an allotment of food from the king's table, which would be like a school food plan during the term of their education. When they have completed their required studies, they will then serve in the government.

It is here that we read of what will come to be known as "the Daniel fast."

> 8But Daniel resolved not to defile himself with the royal food and wine, and he asked the chief official for permission not to defile himself this way. 9Now God had caused the official to show favor and compassion to Daniel, 10but the official told Daniel, "I am afraid of my lord the king, who has assigned your food and drink. Why should he see you looking worse than the other young men your age? The king would then have my head because of you."
>
> 11Daniel then said to the guard whom the chief official had appointed over Daniel,

The New Covenant Fast

Hananiah, Mishael and Azariah, 12"Please test your servants for ten days: Give us nothing but vegetables to eat and water to drink. 13Then compare our appearance with that of the young men who eat the royal food, and treat your servants in accordance with what you see." 14So he agreed to this and tested them for ten days.

15At the end of the ten days they looked healthier and better nourished than any of the young men who ate the royal food. 16So the guard took away their choice food and the wine they were to drink and gave them vegetables instead (Daniel 1:8-16).

With all due respect to those who call this a fast, it does not meet the biblical definition of the Hebrew word *tsum* that is translated into the English word "fast."

Strong's Concordance

***tsum*: to abstain from food, fast**

Original Word: צוּם

Part of Speech: Verb

Transliteration: *tsum*

Phonetic Spelling: (tsoom)

Short Definition: fasted

Daniel is part of the first wave of exiles and has no way possible to ensure that the meats that are being prepared are lawful for him to eat. As a Jew, his foods must be "kosher" in preparation according to the Jewish dietary laws. A vegetarian diet may feel like a fast to a meat eater, but it in no way meets the description of the Hebrew word. I will not introduce any form of fasting that does not fit the biblical description of the word. As the exiled Jews build their communities, they will reconstruct their own ethnicity with shops and foods of their culture and religious beliefs. It will not be long before "kosher" meats will find their way into the marketplace.

I can remember during my teenage years, we felt that if we could liquefy anything in a blender, we were fasting. I must tell you, there were no foods that were off limits to that blender. If you could stomach whatever it was being turned into that unappealing looking slurry, you were good to go; because you were now drinking and not eating. That probably is as good as an example you can get of the religious mind in action, and its attempts to circumvent the heart of the matter. Furthermore, according to the Jewish traditions, only water was permitted during the fast, so despite our efforts, it was no fast at all.

The timeline has moved on, and we find that Daniel has been in Babylon nearly 70 years. He remembers the prophetic words of Jeremiah and the promised return to Israel; he humbles himself before the Lord in prayer and fasting.

> *1In the first year of Darius son of Xerxes (a Mede by descent), who was made ruler over the Babylonian kingdom— 2in the first year of his reign, I, Daniel, understood from the Scriptures, according to the word of the Lord given to Jeremiah the prophet, that the desolation of Jerusalem would last seventy*

years. 3So I turned to the Lord God and pleaded with him in prayer and petition, in fasting, and in sackcloth and ashes.

4I prayed to the Lord my God and confessed:

"Lord, the great and awesome God, who keeps his covenant of love with those who love him and keep his commandments, 5we have sinned and done wrong. We have been wicked and have rebelled; we have turned away from your commands and laws. 6We have not listened to your servants the prophets, who spoke in your name to our kings, our princes and our ancestors, and to all the people of the land.

7"Lord, you are righteous, but this day we are covered with shame—the people of Judah and the inhabitants of Jerusalem and all Israel, both near and far, in all the countries where you have scattered us because of our unfaithfulness to you. 8We and our kings, our princes and our ancestors are covered with shame, Lord, because we have sinned against you. 9The Lord our God is merciful and forgiving, even though we have rebelled against him; 10we have not obeyed the Lord our God or kept the laws he gave us through his servants the prophets. 11All Israel has transgressed your law and turned away, refusing to obey you.

"Therefore the curses and sworn judgments written in the Law of Moses, the servant of God, have been poured out on us, because we have sinned against you. 12You have fulfilled the words spoken against us and against our rulers by bringing on us great disaster. Under the whole heaven nothing has ever been done like what has been done to Jerusalem. 13Just as it is written in the Law of Moses, all this disaster has come on us, yet we have not sought the favor of the Lord our God by turning from our sins and giving attention to your truth. 14The Lord did not hesitate to bring the disaster on us, for the Lord our God is righteous in everything he does; yet we have not obeyed him.

15"Now, Lord our God, who brought your people out of Egypt with a mighty hand and who made for yourself a name that endures to this day, we have sinned, we have done wrong. 16Lord, in keeping with all your righteous acts, turn away your anger and your wrath from Jerusalem, your city, your holy hill. Our sins and the iniquities of our ancestors have made Jerusalem and your people an object of scorn to all those around us.

17"Now, our God, hear the prayers and petitions of your servant. For your sake, Lord, look with favor on your desolate sanctuary. 18Give ear, our God, and hear; open your eyes and see the desolation of the city that bears your Name. We do not make requests of you because we are righteous, but because of your great mercy. 19Lord, listen! Lord, forgive! Lord, hear and act! For your sake, my God, do not

> delay, because your city and your people bear your Name" (Daniel 9:1-19).

It will be through those earnest times of fasting and prayer that we will see the raising up of a leadership from amongst the exiles. They will begin to cry out to the Lord, seeking the freedom to return to their homeland.

The Partial Fast

In this next passage, we will see another reference in regards to Daniel, which has been called by some: "The partial fast."

> *1In the third year of Cyrus king of Persia, a revelation was given to Daniel (who was called Belteshazzar). Its message was true and it concerned a great war. The understanding of the message came to him in a vision.*
>
> *2At that time I, Daniel, mourned for three weeks. 3I ate no choice food; no meat or wine touched my lips; and I used no lotions at all until the three weeks were over* (Daniel 10:1-3).

Certainly, the vision of a great war so troubled Daniel that he humbled himself on that day before the Lord, to learn its interpretation. That day turned into 21 days as he struggled to learn the meaning of the dream. From the very first day of his prayer, the angel of the Lord was sent to him to explain the vision. Had the angel, not been hindered by the spiritual principality over Persia, Daniel would have received the answer from God on the first day. He would have eaten a light meal and that would have been the end of it as it relates to this "so called" fast. This would have barely garnered a footnote in this passage and would have never become a teaching, describing a partial fast.

> *12 Then he continued, "Do not be afraid, Daniel. Since the first day that you set your mind to gain understanding and to humble yourself before your God, your words were heard, and I have come in response to them. 13 But the prince of the Persian kingdom resisted me twenty-one days. Then Michael, one of the chief princes, came to help me, because I was detained there with the king of Persia. 14 Now I have come to explain to you what will happen to your people in the future, for the vision concerns a time yet to come"* (Daniel 10:12-14).

A partial fast would be any part of the day that you consciously abstain from food, miss a meal, and only drink water. This would fit the description of the Hebrew model and word for a fast.

The Fasting Practices of Babylon

The people of Israel and Judah were now scattered throughout Babylon as part of the redistribution of peoples that the Babylonians practiced after their conquests. Only a small percentage were taken as slaves, and it appears that most were allowed to settle in the rich, fertile plains of the Chebar region. They would be allowed to conduct themselves as citizens of Babylon with the rights to farm, conduct business, and trade. The people were permitted to maintain their traditions and practices as long as they were not in conflict with Babylonian law, society or religion. It was expected that they would meld into Babylonian culture and become Babylonians.

While many did, there would emerge a remnant that would struggle to retain their identity and culture as a people. Prophets such as Daniel, Ezekiel, and Zechariah would carry the torch and be a voice for God during the captivity. Jeremiah would be taken against his will with a large group of refugees that fled to Egypt.

The Babylonian religious culture was one of numerous fasts and personal fasts as a part of their penance for any violations against their gods. It's cultural and religious roots came from the Sumerians, but when it was absorbed into the Media-Persian Empire, there was a shift away from public and religious fasting as it was not practiced by the Zoroastrians, better known in biblical circles as "the Magi." This was the religion that had gained prominence under Cyrus' rule. The Sumerian influence on Israel concerning fasting cannot be minimized or dismissed. Prior to captivity while Israel was still in their homeland, the prophet Ezekiel records the abominable practices of worship that took place even in the temple to the false gods of Babylon.

> *12He said to me, "Son of man, have you seen what the elders of Israel are doing in the darkness, each at the shrine of his own idol? They say, 'The Lord does not see us; the Lord has forsaken the land.' 13Again, he said, "You will see them doing things that are even more detestable."*
>
> *14Then he brought me to the entrance of the north gate of the house of the Lord, and I saw women sitting there, mourning the god Tammuz. 15He said to me, "Do you see this, son*

of man? You will see things that are even more detestable than this."

16He then brought me into the inner court of the house of the Lord, and there at the entrance to the temple, between the portico and the altar, were about twenty-five men. With their backs toward the temple of the Lord and their faces toward the east, they were bowing down to the sun in the east.

17He said to me, "Have you seen this, son of man? Is it a trivial matter for the people of Judah to do the detestable things they are doing here? Must they also fill the land with violence and continually arouse my anger? Look at them putting the branch to their nose! 18Therefore I will deal with them in anger; I will not look on them with pity or spare them. Although they shout in my ears, I will not listen to them" (Ezekiel 8:12-18).

The god "Tammuz" was a god that was worshipped by the Babylonians. Each year after the summer solstice, they would have six days of mourning and fasting for this god of food and vegetation, whose "funeral" was held during this time. The death period was the onset of the scorching summer's heat and droughts that were common at that time of the year. You can hear the offense that is felt by God that women in Israel were gathering at the temple gate (verse 14) to mourn this pagan false god. These idolatrous practices that are outlined in this passage led to the prophecies concerning Israel's judgment, and its defeat by the Babylonian Empire.

What seems unusual to this writer is that Israel will drop

names from their calendar and adopt names of the months from the Babylonian calendar. These changes will include the name of the Sumerian god Tammuz for the 6th and 7th month and Sivan, which is the Hindu god Shiva for the 5th and 6th month as it relates to our calendar. The Jews returning from Babylon will have 70 years of Babylonian life and culture, whose influences have permeated their lives.

When Israel departs Babylon and returns to Judea, the nation will have added six new fast days and restructured the Day of Atonement as a part of their religious practice.

Jewish Fast Days

According to Rabbinic teachings, the act of fasting was based upon three positions of the heart.

1. An act of contrition to God for sins that had been committed.
2. An act of commemorative mourning
3. An act of commemorative gratitude

These added fast days would comprise one or more of these aspects of their tradition.

The Fast of Gedaliah

This commemoration was considered a minor fast day, which concluded by the evening of the same day. It is for the remembrance of the assassinated governor of Judah, whose name was Gedaliah. He presided over the remaining Jews left in the land after the destruction of Jerusalem by the Babylonians. The purpose of this fast was to remember the destruction of the temple and his life with prayer and the reading of the Torah.

The Fast of the 10th of Tevet

The purpose of this fast was to remember the siege of Jerusalem by the Babylonians and was again a minor fast day from sunrise to sunset. You could work on this day but it was to be a day of soul-searching and examining your relationship with God. The 10th day of Tevet never falls on the Sabbath, so fasting is always permitted.

Maimonides, the noted Rabbi of the Middle Ages wrote, "The essential significance of the fast of the Tenth of Tevet, as well as that of the other fast days, is not primarily the grief and mourning which they evoke. Their aim is rather to awaken the hearts towards repentance; to recall to us, both the evil deeds of our fathers and our own evil deeds, which caused anguish to befall both them and us and thereby to cause us to return towards the good."

The Fast of the 17th of Tammuz

This fast commemorates the breach of the walls of Jerusalem by Nebuchadnezzar's army leading up to the destruction of the temple. This again is a minor day of fasting and takes place from sunrise to sunset. It is considered to be a time of mourning and sadness.

The Fast of Tisha B'av

This fast is to commemorate the tragedies that had befallen Israel. It begins with the destruction of the first temple and the exile to Babylon. It continues through its history as a people. It is a 25-hour fast and is conducted with the reading of the book of Lamentations written by the prophet Jeremiah.

The Fast of Esther

This fast was to commemorate the story of Purim, which is the biblical account from the book of Esther. Israel was delivered from the plot of Haman to destroy the Jews still living within the Persian Empire. The fast was in commemoration of Esther's call to the Jews in the city of Susa for fasting on her behalf.

The Fast of the Firstborn

This fast of gratitude was initiated in the post-captivity period. It was to commemorate the saving of the Israelite firstborn during the judgment of all the firstborn in Egypt as recorded in the book of Exodus. This fast was from sunrise to sunset and was conducted the day before the Passover.

It should be noted that none of these fasts are ordained by Scripture. They became a part of Judaism and their religious culture that was brought back to Israel, even after the edict of Cyrus, who allowed the Jews to return to their homeland.

The Day of Atonement

It should be also noted that the Day of Atonement was changed to become a day of fasting with its prescribed ritual during the exile period. This was done to maintain the observance of the day in absence of the temple and its required sacrifice.

I will repeat the tradition as described in Chapter one. Incense would be burned instead of a sacrificial burnt offering. As outlined in the Talmud, they then enacted new regulations that were put in place for its observance. They wrote that in the absence of a temple, five afflictions are required:

1. No food or water during the 25-hour period.
2. No wearing of leather shoes.
3. No anointing oneself with oil.
4. No bathing.
5. No marital relations.

Once again, make no mistake concerning the Talmud; this is not Scripture. Jesus called these rules adopted by the religious leaders of Israel "as the traditions of men."

Ezra and Nehemiah

On the decree of Cyrus, King of Persia, permission was granted for the Jews to return to their native land to rebuild the temple. Ezra will lead the first wave of returning exiles along with the prophets Haggai and Zechariah. From reading the book of Ezra, you gain a real sense of the heart of this leader who is looking to God for guidance every step of the way. He is facing monumental challenges of moving man and material to a land that he has only heard about and has never seen. In humility, with fasting and prayer over concern for the integrity and honor of God, the people come before the Lord.

> *21There, by the Ahava Canal, I proclaimed a fast, so that we might humble ourselves before our God and ask him for a safe journey for us and our children, with all our possessions. 22I was ashamed to ask the king for soldiers and horsemen to protect us from enemies on the road, because we had told the king, "The gracious hand of our God is on everyone who looks to him, but his great anger is against all who forsake him." 23So we fasted and petitioned our God about this, and he answered*

our prayer (Ezra 8:21-23).

After returning to Judea, the first waves of exiles are facing enormous challenges within and threats from those without. These hindrances halt the construction on the temple.

Nehemiah lives in the royal city of Susa and serves as the king's cupbearer. He hears from the exiles of the great difficulties that they are facing in trying to rebuild the temple while the walls of Jerusalem are broken down. They are under constant threat and danger from those who want the work stopped. In mourning, with fasting and prayer, he makes his petition before the Lord seeking God's direction. King Artaxerxes grants Nehemiah a temporary leave of absence to oversee the rebuilding of the walls of Jerusalem under extremely difficult circumstances.

Once the walls were completed, Ezra gathered all of the people together to worship the Lord and hear the reading of the Law of Moses. One can only imagine the emotion of that day as the people gathered together and began to weep and mourn. It was then that Nehemiah and Ezra proclaimed to them that this was a time of celebration and feasting, not a time of mourning. It is from this passage that we get that beloved scripture quote, "The joy of the Lord is our strength." What began with weeping turned into a seven-day celebration.

I find it rather odd that the next recorded fast comes a few days after this call to celebrate. One of the required fast days of the seventh month was now upon them. The leadership, in following the traditions that they had learned in Babylon, committed themselves as a people to fast. They covered themselves in sackcloth and ashes as they renewed their vows to the Lord. Zechariah will speak to the nation on these issues. He will deliver the word of the Lord in the form of a rebuke and a promised blessing.

The Prophet Zechariah

While the people of Israel were in the process of adapting their lives spiritually and physically in their new environment, God was not silent. The prophet Zechariah is calling out to Israel to return to the Lord with the promise of a return of God's favor and blessings. The time period is about 520 BC or 3240 on the Hebrew calendar and the people of Israel had started returning to the land in stages since 537 BC. Zechariah would be among one of the first groups that would make the long trip home to Israel.

The returning exiles inquired of the Lord whether they should continue the fasts that were done in the 5th month, which was the fast of Tisha B'av. This fast was to mourn the tragedies that had befallen Israel; you can understand why they were asking the question. This was a time of great joy for the people of Israel and Judah because they were returning to their homeland. Notice how the Lord responds to their question in the following passage.

> 1In the fourth year of King Darius, the word of the Lord came to Zechariah on the fourth day of the ninth month, the month of Kislev. 2The people of Bethel had sent Sharezer and Regem-Melek, together with their men, to entreat the Lord 3by asking the priests of the house of the Lord Almighty and the prophets, "Should I mourn and fast in the fifth month, as I have done for so many years?"
>
> 4Then the word of the Lord Almighty came to

me: 5"Ask all the people of the land and the priests, 'When you fasted and mourned in the fifth and seventh months for the past seventy years, was it really for me that you fasted? 6And when you were eating and drinking, were you not just feasting for yourselves? 7Are these not the words the Lord proclaimed through the earlier prophets when Jerusalem and its surrounding towns were at rest and prosperous, and the Negev and the western foothills were settled?' 8And the word of the Lord came again to Zechariah: 9"This is what the Lord Almighty said: 'Administer true justice; show mercy and compassion to one another. 10Do not oppress the widow or the fatherless, the foreigner or the poor. Do not plot evil against each other.'

11"But they refused to pay attention; stubbornly they turned their backs and covered their ears. 12They made their hearts as hard as flint and would not listen to the law or to the words that the Lord Almighty had sent by his Spirit through the earlier prophets. So the Lord Almighty was very angry.

13"When I called, they did not listen; so when they called, I would not listen,' says the Lord Almighty. 14'I scattered them with a whirlwind among all the nations, where they were strangers. The land they left behind them was so desolate that no one traveled through it. This is how they made the pleasant land desolate'" (Zechariah 7:1-14).

Unlike what they thought, God was never interested in their fasts or their ritual feasts; He was interested in the state of their hearts. God wanted His people to show mercy, compassion, and true justice to one another; instead, he was served a ritual from a hardened heart. Zechariah then prophesies encouragement to the people to rebuild the temple and their lives as God has turned to them once again with favor. God did not want their fasts; He wanted a celebration for His people marking their return to God.

> 18The word of the Lord Almighty came to me.
>
> 19This is what the Lord Almighty says: "The fasts of the fourth, fifth, seventh and tenth months will become joyful and glad occasions and happy festivals for Judah. Therefore love truth and peace."
>
> 20This is what the Lord Almighty says: "Many peoples and the inhabitants of many cities will yet come, 21and the inhabitants of one city will go to another and say, 'Let us go at once to entreat the Lord and seek the Lord Almighty. I myself am going.' 22And many peoples and powerful nations will come to Jerusalem to seek the Lord Almighty and to entreat him."
>
> 23This is what the Lord Almighty says: "In those days ten people from all languages and nations will take firm hold of one Jew by the hem of his robe and say, 'Let us go with you, because we have heard that God is with you"

(Zechariah 8:18-23).

Zechariah's prophetic word will go unheeded as Israel would

maintain those fast days. To this day, they are still observed in some parts of Orthodox Judaism.

Esther

Meanwhile back in Susa, which was the seat of power for the Persian Empire, a new threat emerges. The Jewish people that have remained in Babylon along with the other nations now under Persian rule will face a new threat of extermination. Haman, who was a high-ranking official within the government, has convinced the King to enact laws that will subsequently entrap the Jewish people and subject them to a sentence of death. Esther, who had been made queen, will call for a 3-day fast of no food or water for all Jews living in Susa as she risks her life by approaching the king without being summoned. The people are horrified at the news, and they cry out to the Lord with great weeping and wailing, covering themselves in sackcloth and ashes. The wicked plot by Haman will be exposed and a new law will be enacted for the self-protection of all Jews. It will be from this near fateful event that the Feast of Purim and the Fast of Esther will become part of the Jewish tradition.

Israel Reborn as a Nation

The rebuilt walls of Jerusalem signal a time of resettlement for this great and historic city. The nation has been unified again as one people but is still ruled by a foreign government. Israel is allowed once again to worship the God of their fathers and will reintroduce the practices of temple worship. It is after this period that we see the rise of the Empire of Greece threatening the many years of peace that Israel has enjoyed as Alexander the Great makes war with the Persians. His armies will move through Judea in 332 BC and leave behind Greek culture with its philosophies, politics and religions. The armies of Greece and her allies will sweep through the Fertile Crescent from Egypt to the Indus Valley and beyond conquering every nation in its path.

The time of peace will be shattered during the rule of Antiochus IV, the eighth ruler of the Seleucid Empire. His hatred of the Jewish religion and its culture was at the heart of his desire to completely Hellenize Israel. During this period, Israel had a large percentage of its population that resembled the Greeks more than its own heritage. This was not enough for this ruler who claimed that he was "the visible god."

When there was resistance to the wholesale exchange from Jewish culture and religion to that of Greek Hellenism, Antiochus IV went into a rage. He sent his armies from Syria, destroyed Jerusalem, and crushed the opposition with the help of Hellenist Jews. Only those Jews willing to adopt Greek culture could remain in Jerusalem and Judaism was outlawed. A statue of the Greek god Jupiter was placed in the temple, and a pig was sacrificed on its altar; all of this took place in 168 BC. This triggered a war known as the Maccabean Revolt, which lasted from 167 BC to 160 BC. The continued struggle by the Maccabees would eventually bring forth Israel's independence in 143 BC.

The Roman Empire defeated the Greeks and became the new dominant force in the earth. They then moved into the land of Israel in 63 BC, which set the political, cultural, and religious setting into which Jesus made His entrance in the world.

On a far lesser note, Hippocrates, who would be known as the father of modern medicine wrote this famous quote in regards to fasting as a cure for sickness:

The Physician Within

"Everyone has a physician inside him or her; we just have to help it in its work. The natural healing force within each one of us is the greatest force in getting well. Our food should be our medicine. Our medicine should be our food. But to eat when you are sick is to feed your sickness" – Hippocrates 460-370 BC

The Silence is Deafening

Malachi will be the last prophetic voice in Israel and his last prophecy will herald the coming of one like Elijah who will prepare the way of the Lord. That person was John the Baptist. It will mark a silent period between these prophets of over 400 years. Malachi's prophetic book was written in the year 430 BC or the year 3330 on the Jewish calendar.

Chapter 4

The Messiah Has Come

By the time Jesus enters humanity, a culture of fasting has enveloped Israel. While Israel was in exile in Babylon, the religious leaders enacted several fasts to be observed while in captivity and continued them even after their return to their homeland. The Pharisees were now fasting twice a week, and it was deemed to be a high form of piety. The prophetic voice has been silent for over four hundred years and the Jewish religion has taken a course of strict ritual that can completely function on its own in the absence of God. The nation is under the occupation of the Roman Empire, and they govern Israel with an iron fist. The Jewish Independence movement has brought conflict and instability to the region and this has resulted in a harsh, quick, and violent response by the Roman military. Israel will be one large problem area in an era otherwise known as the "Pax Romana" or "Roman Peace."

During this period, it will be known as a time of great prosperity and Israel will enjoy a share of this economic growth even in the midst of the growing underlying tension and hostility. The nation will be strongly influenced by three groups vying for the loyalty of its citizens. The wealthy elite who work with Rome and want to maintain the status quo and the religious establishment will try to share governance and rule under Rome. Lastly, the Zealot movement wants the overthrow of Roman rule through war or any other means possible. This will be the backdrop as Jesus enters the scene and proclaims the Isaiah 61 mandate of the Messiah.

Jesus Fasts 40 Days

> *"Then Jesus was led up by the Spirit into the wilderness to be tempted by the devil. 2And after fasting forty days and forty nights, he was hungry. 3And the tempter came and said to him"* (Matthew 3:1-3a).

> *"Jesus, full of the Holy Spirit, left the Jordan and was led by the Spirit into the wilderness, 2where for forty days he was tempted by the devil. He ate nothing during those days, and at the end of them he was hungry"* (Luke 4:1).

Matthew's account of Jesus and His 40-day fast implies that after He completed it and was hungry, Satan came to tempt Him. Luke's account suggests that the temptation took place during the forty days of the fast and continued immediately after it. In Mark's gospel, he adds that Jesus would be in the wilderness during that period among the wild animals. Whatever the temptations were during His fasting period, it is clear by the scripture's emphasis that those that came directly after His fast were for the benefit of our instruction. We will return to this subject shortly, but I would like to focus first on the spiritual dynamics of Jesus' fast.

Jesus Reclaims Mankind's Destiny

There is an important underlying act in Jesus entering into His 40-day fast, which needs to be addressed. Everything that

Moses brought forth, Jesus would do likewise, in order to fulfill and bring it to completion. To the dotting of all of the "i's" and the crossing of all of the "t's," the Law of Moses would find its legal requirement satisfied, and its judgment against mankind served at the cross of Christ. Jesus must fulfill every prophetic word that was spoken concerning the Messiah and everything would be completed to perfection. I believe this forty-day fast was to reset through prayer, the invitation that was made by God to His people at Mount Sinai some 1470 years prior, which led to Moses' first fast.

Israel had turned down that invitation to be a nation, whereby, every person would be a priest before God. It was in response to their collective "no" that Moses goes up into the mountain and receives in detail what is known as the Law of Moses and the design for the tabernacle and its contents.

I cannot emphasize enough how important this is from the heart of God and for each and every believer. Jesus would reclaim the invitation from the Father that all of His people, every single one, would be a priest before Him. What that invitation meant was that every person could go directly before God with Jesus being the sole mediator for mankind. Through Jesus, we have unlimited and immediate access to the Father. We need no other person to go through in order to worship and serve our God. The Lord desires intimacy with His people to share His thoughts with and to reveal His heart to you, His beloved. I wonder how the Father's heart must have been grieved on that day when Israel rejected this offer.

On that day, as told in the book of Exodus, all Israel agreed to the offer of being a nation of priests, but then changed their minds. They witnessed the awesome presence of God at Mount Sinai. Moses had seen a burning bush, but they were witnessing the entire mountain being enveloped in fire. They would also see something like a descending ramp that looked like it was made of sapphire and on it stood the form of a man. They had seen the cloud of His presence cover the mountain and witnessed the lightning and thunder within it. Now they heard the audible voice of God deliver the commandments. This proved all too much for them, and they told Moses that they no longer wanted to accept the offer of being a priesthood nation before God. The following is the account of that event:

> 3Then Moses went up to God, and the Lord called to him from the mountain and said, "This is what you are to say to the descendants of Jacob and what you are to tell the people of Israel: 4'You yourselves have seen what I did to Egypt, and how I carried you on eagles wings and brought you to myself. 5Now if you obey me fully and keep my covenant, then out of all nations you will be my treasured possession. Although the whole earth is mine, 6you will be for me a kingdom of priests and a holy nation.' These are the words you are to speak to the Israelites."
>
> 7So Moses went back and summoned the elders of the people and set before them all the words the Lord had commanded him to speak. 8The people all responded together, "We will do everything the Lord has said." So Moses brought their answer back to the Lord.

9The Lord said to Moses, "I am going to come to you in a dense cloud, so that the people will hear me speaking with you and will always put their trust in you." Then Moses told the Lord what the people had said.

10And the Lord said to Moses, "Go to the people and consecrate them today and tomorrow. Have them wash their clothes 11and be ready by the third day, because on that day the Lord will come down on Mount Sinai in the sight of all the people. 12Put limits for the people around the mountain and tell them, 'Be careful that you do not approach the mountain or touch the foot of it. Whoever touches the mountain is to be put to death. 13They are to be stoned or shot with arrows; not a hand is to be laid on them. No person or animal shall be permitted to live.' Only when the ram's horn sounds a long blast may they approach the mountain."

14After Moses had gone down the mountain to the people, he consecrated them, and they washed their clothes. 15Then he said to the people, "Prepare yourselves for the third day. Abstain from sexual relations."

16On the morning of the third day there was thunder and lightning, with a thick cloud over the mountain, and a very loud trumpet blast. Everyone in the camp trembled. 17Then Moses led the people out of the camp to meet with God, and they stood at the foot of the *mountain. 18Mount Sinai was covered with smoke, because the Lord descended on it in fire. The smoke billowed up from it like smoke from a furnace, and the whole mountain trembled violently. 19As the sound of the trumpet grew louder and louder, Moses spoke and the voice of God answered him.*

20The Lord descended to the top of Mount Sinai and called Moses to the top of the mountain (Exodus 19:3-20)

18When the people saw the thunder and lightning and heard the trumpet and saw the mountain in smoke, they trembled with fear. They stayed at a distance 19and said to Moses, "Speak to us yourself and we will listen. But do not have God speak to us or we will die."

20Moses said to the people, "Do not be afraid. God has come to test you, so that the fear of God will be with you to keep you from sinning."

21The people remained at a distance, while Moses approached the thick darkness where God was (Exodus 20:18-21).

8Moses then took the blood, sprinkled it on the people and said, "This is the blood of the covenant that the Lord has made with you in accordance with all these words."

9Moses and Aaron, Nadab and Abihu, and the seventy elders of Israel went up 10and saw the God of Israel. Under his feet was something like a pavement made of lapis lazuli, as bright blue as the sky. 11But God did not raise his hand against these leaders of the Israelites; they saw God, and they ate and drank.

12The Lord said to Moses, "Come up to me on the mountain and stay here, and I will give you the tablets of stone with the law and commandments I have written for their instruction."

13Then Moses set out with Joshua his aide, and Moses went up on the mountain of God (Exodus 24:8-13).

When you think about that offer made by God, your mind can only wonder what direction the course of history might have taken if Israel had said, "yes" to God. The Levites as a tribe would have seen their role dramatically changed within the nation. If the entire population were priests, then on whose behalf would they be ministering to the Lord? Would the mystery of the gospel as the apostle Paul calls it, be revealed that all mankind can know the Father and that the Messiah is God for all nations? Would the Gentiles be the people this priesthood nation serves to proclaim the Good News to them? What would become of the future temple, the sacrificial offerings, the Levitical requirements and the details of the Law of Moses? And most importantly, how would Jesus pay the price of sin for all mankind? At that point in history, none of the books of the Bible were written, a whole new history could have been told. Was it Jesus who was standing on the sapphire ramp? Would He have made Himself known at that time? One can only speculate as to the "what ifs" that could have unfolded on that day of decision.

This epic, holy event ends with a covenant meal being eaten before God with Moses and the elders of Israel beholding this awesome and terrifying display of God's glory. It is also important to note that it was a meal and not a fast that took place. It is from this backdrop that Moses goes up into the mountain to receive the blueprints of the covenant, its ordinances, the temple design and the Ten Commandments written in stone.

The Blueprints of the New Covenant

Jesus enters into His fast, not solely to be tempted of the Devil, for the scripture says that the main confrontation with Satan occurred after He completed the fast. So what was the purpose of Jesus and His 40-day fast in the wilderness?

I believe there was more than just returning to that place in the Spirit before God to receive again the offer of a priesthood nation. Moses, while on his fast received exacting details of the tabernacle right down to the eye loops for the curtains; nothing was left to the whim of man in its design. In the symbolic allegory of this event, I see Jesus in vivid detail – seeing every part of the temple of the New Covenant that He would build. It wasn't made of stone and materials but, in fact, it was made of living stones that the Father would give Him. Jesus would be praying and seeing all who would ever come to know Him. He would continue to do so during His earthly ministry as told in the passage from the gospel of John.

> *"I pray for them. I am not praying for the world, but for those you have given me, for they are yours. 10All I have is yours, and all you have is mine. And glory has come to me through them"* (John 17:9,10).

If Jesus was seeing His temple during that forty-day fast, then He was seeing you, me, and every other living stone that the Father was giving Him. You would be always in His heart, mind, and prayer just as He prayed for us all on the night of His arrest. It gives me great comfort to know that the Lord knew me before I was born. His interest was not reserved for some elite saint, but for everyone who belongs to Him. And O' how precious you are in His sight; you are known of Him even before the foundation of the world. Just as Moses received the blueprint for the Old Covenant, Jesus completes His fast with His Father's blueprint of the New Covenant written on His heart.

Jesus Redeems the Birthright of Mankind

It is at this point after He completes the fast that Satan tries to tempt Jesus in His hunger to deliver Himself with a creative miracle.

> "The devil said to him, "If you are the Son of God, tell this stone to become bread."4Jesus answered, "It is written: 'Man shall not live on bread alone'" (Luke 4:3, 4).

In the ancient world, bread and life were synonymous with one another. What Satan offers as life is nothing more than a lifeless stone. Bread can sustain a man for a time but the Word of God sustains a man for all eternity. Jesus is the Word made flesh. He is the Bread of Life, and He breaks the fast of desperate and starving mankind.

> The devil led him up to a high place and showed him in an instant all the kingdoms of the world. 6And he said to him, 'I will give you all their authority and splendor; it has been

given to me, and I can give it to anyone I want to. 7If you worship me, it will all be yours.' 8Jesus answered, "It is written: 'Worship the Lord your God and serve him only' (Luke 4:5-8).

Jesus will answer the Devil's questions from the book of Deuteronomy, from the law that was given to Moses while He was on Mount Sinai. Satan then thinks that He is offering Jesus something bigger than that which God has given Him. He offers Jesus the world.

Satan is not omniscient, in other words, he's not all-knowing. What he knows is from what he has learned in the past and what he gathers currently as intelligence from man. Israel had a belief that went something like this: Messiah will set up an earthly kingdom from which He will rule Israel in peace and prosperity, and it will be something like heaven on the earth. Oh and P.S. — no Gentiles allowed. If this is what man believed, then that was the extent of the knowledge that Satan knew. The Devil had no idea of what Paul called "The Mystery of the Gospel." He would never know about it until after the fact that it was Messiah's purpose to redeem all of mankind, not just the Jews. Paul reveals this through the following passage in his letter to the Corinthians and the Ephesians.

No, we declare God's wisdom, a mystery that has been hidden and that God destined for our glory before time began. 8None of the rulers of this age understood it, for if they had, they would not have crucified the Lord of glory. 9However, as it is written: "What no eye has seen, what no ear has heard, and what no

> human mind has conceived"—the things God has prepared for those who love him— 10these are the things God has revealed to us by his Spirit (1 Corinthians 2:7-10).

> "This mystery is that through the gospel the Gentiles are heirs together with Israel, members together of one body, and sharers together in the promise in Christ Jesus" (Ephesians 3:6).

So, what Satan thought was the "big offer" was, in fact, no offer at all. Jesus was to receive the entire world as His reward. Jesus was recovering the priesthood nation that Israel had turned down, but this time, He would restore it for all mankind.

Think about that for a moment. If Satan had known God's plan of salvation, his strategy would have changed to ensure that Jesus would not sacrifice His life as an offering for all mankind. The Devil would have enlisted every demon to make sure that Jesus would not have His life imperiled. By doing so, he would preserve his kingdom of darkness. It is for that reason that the mystery of the gospel remained hidden in the words of the prophets, and Jesus could fulfill the plan of God with some measure of stealth. Salvation is offered to the entire world, to as many as will receive Him. As part of the inheritance of the saints, they have the privilege of being recognized as priests before God Almighty.

> Grace and peace to you from him who is, and who was, and who is to come, and from the seven spirits before his throne, 5and from Jesus Christ, who is the faithful witness, the firstborn from the dead, and the ruler of the kings of the

> earth. To him who loves us and has freed us from our sins by his blood, 6and has made us to be a kingdom and priests to serve his God and Father—to him be glory and power forever and ever! Amen (Revelation 1:4-6).

Our God is an awesome God!

> 9The devil led him to Jerusalem and had him stand on the highest point of the temple. "If you are the Son of God," he said, "throw yourself down from here. 10For it is written:
>
> "'He will command his angels concerning you to guard you carefully; 11they will lift you up in their hands, so that you will not strike your foot against a stone.'" 12Jesus answered, "It is said: 'Do not put the Lord your God to the test.'" 13When the devil had finished all this tempting, he left him until an opportune time (Luke 4:9-13).

Lastly, Satan pathetically tries to entice Jesus to put on a show to prove His deity. He would employ this tactic throughout Jesus' earthly ministry to no avail. The entrance for all mankind into the kingdom of God will be by grace through faith. Jesus was proving who He was throughout His ministry by His works of healings, signs, and wonders. He would tell the people that His works testify who He was, just as Isaiah 61 prophesied what the Messiah would do. Those who could see would believe on Jesus, those who could not, remained spiritually blind. Unbelief kept them bound in the prison of their own hardened hearts. Jesus had no need to put the Father to the test to receive acknowledgement from anyone, let alone that fallen creature.

At the end of the temptation, Jesus had redeemed the failure of Adam and Eve in Genesis 3:6 when they succumbed in the Garden to the same three points of lure: the lust of the flesh, the lust of the eyes, and the pride of life.

> *"When the woman saw that the fruit of the tree was good for food and pleasing to the eye, and also desirable for gaining wisdom, she took some and ate it. She also gave some to her husband, who was with her, and he ate it"* (Genesis 3:6).

Satan had tempted Jesus with the lust of the flesh by trying to get Him to satisfy His physical need by creating bread. He had failed to tempt Jesus with the lust of the eyes by showing and offering Him all the kingdoms of the world and their glory, which Jesus flatly turned down. And lastly, he tried to tempt Jesus with the pride of life by imploring Him to leap off a building to flaunt His deity in a vain show of glory. Jesus is leaving no stone unturned in reclaiming our birthright for us by retracing all of the steps that have brought man to this fallen place. He restores it for mankind with His sinless life.

> *Do not love the world or anything in the world. If anyone loves the world, love for the Father is not in them. 16For everything in the world—the lust of the flesh, the lust of the eyes, and the pride of life—comes not from the Father but from the world. 17The world and its desires pass away, but whoever does the will of God lives forever* (1 John 2:15-17).

When you look at the fasts of Moses and Jesus in allegory, you can see how critically important Jesus' fast was on behalf of His future priesthood nation. Just as Moses was given every detail of the tabernacle, Jesus saw every detail of His temple of living stones and where they were to be placed in Him. Just as Moses received the Law written in stone, Jesus embodied the royal Law, which was "love one another." Everything that Moses received that ushered in the Old Covenant, Jesus would embody in the New Covenant. He would know in detail the high cost that He would have to pay through His death and resurrection. If this is the temptation that He faced during His fast, then it was seeing in detail all that He would have to suffer. He would see what must transpire in order to bring to pass His beloved future priesthood nation. I do not know what could be a worse temptation than seeing everything you must suffer in the spirit and then have to be willing to live it out in the natural realm.

Thank You, our precious Savior; for all You have done for us, we are so very thankful.

This will be the only recorded fast by Jesus in Scripture. Moses, Elijah, and Jesus will have conducted 40-day fasts and will appear together at the Mount of Transfiguration. Moses and Elijah representing the Old Covenant law and prophets and Jesus transitioning the world to a new and better covenant built upon better promises.

> 5They serve at a sanctuary that is a copy and shadow of what is in heaven. This is why Moses was warned when he was about to build the tabernacle: "See to it that you make everything according to the pattern shown you on the mountain." 6But in fact the ministry Jesus has received is as superior to theirs as the covenant of which he is mediator is superior to the old

one, since the new covenant is established on better promises. 7For if there had been nothing wrong with that first covenant, no place would have been sought for another (Hebrews 8:5-7).

"By calling this covenant "new," he has made the first one obsolete; and what is obsolete and outdated will soon disappear" (Hebrews 8:13

The year is approximately 27 AD or the year 3787 on the Hebrew calendar.

Chapter 5

The Verse that Never Was

When the Lord brought up the subject of fasting to me, I felt quite certain in my beliefs. I had pictured in my mind, that fasting was similar to bringing in the heavy artillery into the battle. In Matthew, Mark, and Luke's gospels, they write concerning a boy and his violent seizures and the disciple's inability to heal him. I was certain that this passage would be my sure defense and would validate my held belief. This will soundly prove that fasting supercharges prayer and that would be my "seal the doctrinal deal" or so I thought. So let's read all three passages that relate to this story and examine the scriptures carefully.

So here's the backdrop to the story: Jesus takes with Him, Peter, James, and John up into the mountain to pray. They would end up spending the night there, and the other nine disciples would spend the night in the town below. The story would come to be known as the Mount of Transfiguration. Moses and Elijah have appeared to speak to a transfigured Jesus in all His glory about His impending death. Peter, James, and John witness Jesus in a glory so radiant that if there was a glory on Moses or Elijah, it was unremarkable. Peter wants to make three booths or monuments to mark the occasion. As he voices his ideas, God interrupts him audibly by saying "This is my beloved Son, hear Him." When the disciples hear the audible voice of God, they fall down and lay prostrate on the ground. Jesus tells them to get up and to not be afraid. When they open their eyes, only Jesus remains, and He tells them that they were not to repeat what they have seen until after His resurrection. In the morning, they leave that awesome place of prayer and head down the mountain to join the rest of the disciples. When they meet them, they enter a situation that is in utter chaos.

> 14When they came to the crowd, a man approached Jesus and knelt before him. 15"Lord, have mercy on my son," he said. "He has seizures and is suffering greatly. He often falls into the fire or into the water. 16I brought him to your disciples, but they could not heal him."
>
> 17 "You unbelieving and perverse generation," Jesus replied, "how long shall I stay with you? How long shall I put up with you? Bring the boy here to me." 18Jesus rebuked the demon, and it came out of the boy, and he was healed at that moment.
>
> 19Then the disciples came to Jesus in private and asked, "Why couldn't we drive it out?"
>
> 20He replied, "Because you have so little faith. Truly I tell you, if you have faith as small as a mustard seed, you can say to this mountain, 'Move from here to there,' and it will move. Nothing will be impossible for you." 21 (Verse 21 is omitted in the New International Version) (Matthew 17:14-21).

The Verse that Never Was

"Howbeit this kind goeth not out but by prayer and fasting" (Matthew 17:21, KJV).

14When they came to the other disciples, they saw a large crowd around them and the teachers of the law arguing with them. 15As soon as all the people saw Jesus, they were overwhelmed with wonder and ran to greet him.

16 "What are you arguing with them about?" he asked.

17A man in the crowd answered, "Teacher, I brought you my son, who is possessed by a spirit that has robbed him of speech. 18Whenever it seizes him, it throws him to the ground. He foams at the mouth, gnashes his teeth and becomes rigid. I asked your disciples to drive out the spirit, but they could not."

19 "You unbelieving generation," Jesus replied, "how long shall I stay with you? How long shall I put up with you? Bring the boy to me."

20So they brought him. When the spirit saw Jesus, it immediately threw the boy into a convulsion. He fell to the ground and rolled around, foaming at the mouth.

21Jesus asked the boy's father, "How long has he been like this?"

"From childhood," he answered. 22"It has often thrown him into fire or water to kill him. But if you can do anything, take pity on us and help

us."

23 "If you can'?" said Jesus. "Everything is possible for one who believes."

24Immediately the boy's father exclaimed, "I do believe; help me overcome my unbelief!"

25When Jesus saw that a crowd was running to the scene, he rebuked the impure spirit. "You deaf and mute spirit," he said, "I command you, come out of him and never enter him again."

26The spirit shrieked, convulsed him violently and came out. The boy looked so much like a corpse that many said, "He's dead." 27But Jesus took him by the hand and lifted him to his feet, and he stood up.

28After Jesus had gone indoors, his disciples asked him privately, "Why couldn't we drive it out?"

29He replied, "This kind can come out only by prayer" (Mark 9:14-29).

"And he said unto them, This kind can come forth by nothing, but by prayer and fasting" (Mark 9:29, KJV).

37The next day, when they came down from the mountain, a large crowd met him. 38A man in the crowd called out, "Teacher, I beg you to look at my son, for he is my only child. 39A spirit seizes him and he suddenly screams; it throws him into convulsions so that he foams at the mouth. It scarcely ever leaves him and is destroying him. 40I begged your disciples to drive it out, but they could not."

41 "You unbelieving and perverse generation," Jesus replied, "how long shall I stay with you and put up with you? Bring your son here."

42Even while the boy was coming, the demon threw him to the ground in a convulsion. But Jesus rebuked the impure spirit, healed the boy and gave him back to his father. 43And they were all amazed at the greatness of God (Luke 9:37-43).

I have laid out all three passages so that we can round out the story, add further light as to what is transpiring, and then piece it all together. So, let's pick up this passage from where I previously left off. Jesus returns from the mountain with Peter, James, and John, and they come back to the village and witness a chaotic scene taking place.

A large crowd has gathered to watch this spectacle that has the nine disciples arguing and in a debate with the Pharisees and Sadducees over the reasons why the child is not healed. The father of the young boy asked the disciples to heal and deliver his son from these horrific seizures, but they cannot help the child. The father then sees Jesus and asks Him if He can do anything? Jesus responds by calling the people of His day, an unbelieving and perverse generation; He takes control of the situation. He moves away from the crowd to speak to the father and brings the child over to Him away from all of the commotion. He calms down the entire scene and addresses the condition of the father's belief. Afterward, He interviews him about his son's history of the illness.

The crowd sees Jesus and starts running toward Him, but before they get to Him, Jesus speaks with authority and casts the spirit out of the child; the seizure ceases immediately, and the child is rescued from his horrible ordeal. Order is restored; the child is healed and delivered and a family is relieved of the trauma that they have undergone. They have had to watch their son suffer repeatedly and felt completely helpless to do anything about it. Afterward, the disciples ask Jesus why they could not do anything for the child.

Now, before we discuss the disciple's question, let's retrace our steps to what Jesus had to say during that dramatic event. The father of the boy asks Jesus if He can do anything to help his child. Jesus replies: "**if I can**?" He then says to him "**if you can** believe, nothing will be impossible to you." All three gospels agree that the context of this story is about believing faith. This is an important key when studying the Bible because in identifying the heart of the passage, you establish the base of understanding that God intended for that passage. So remember this key, "the context is the context." Once you identify the center or core thought and establish the context of a passage, then you can add the sub plots and sub thoughts around the core message.

So, in this passage, Jesus has declared that the issue that has kept the child from being delivered is unbelief. When the father asks Jesus if He can do anything, Jesus places the question solely back on the father. This is not about religious issues of who's at fault for the child's condition. Although, I am sure that was at the core of the debate between the disciples and the religious leaders. It wasn't even about the disciples. For Jesus doesn't even point to them as being relevant to the discussion He is having with the parent. It wasn't about who prayed or who fasted. The focus of the

Lord's attention is on what the parent of this child believes. It is at this moment an honest heart-cry from the man emerges to the Lord: "I believe, help my unbelief."

Jesus stated that the people of His day were perverse and unbelieving. By saying "this generation," He has indicted everyone at this scene. In the Lord's confrontations with the Pharisees and Sadducees, He will hold them accountable for this culture of unbelief that their teachings have fostered. So why would Jesus say such a harsh thing like that in earshot of everyone? The reason why unbelief is such a perversion of truth is because it holds in its core belief that the power of evil as in this particular case is something greater than the power of God.

Unconsciously and subtly, it deems that Satan's power is greater than God's. Make no mistake about this: unbelief **is** a belief. The "un" is just the direction of where that belief is traveling — opposite to, and away from God. Think about how offensive that must be to our heavenly Father. As I said, I do not think that the Lord was sparing anyone when He said those words, not the religious leaders, not the immediate family, not the crowd and not even His own disciples.

If you have ever been in a ministry situation like that, you know how easily you can move from faith when you encounter such an overt manifestation as had happened in that boy. You have to choose not to be distracted by what you see and hear. You must steel your inner man in faith, and resolve for that person's sake, to keep at bay all fear and distraction.

The gospels vary in their account of Jesus' response to the disciples asking why they could not help the boy: Luke makes no mention of the interaction between Jesus and the disciples. Mark relates that Jesus says that prayer is the issue and in Matthew, the controversial "prayer and fasting" verse is omitted by most modern translations except for those that try to stay true to the King James Version. For someone like me who has used the King James Version and then later adopted the New King James Version as my primary source of study for over 40 years, I was oblivious to the fact that there was an issue with Matthew 17:21. I would boldly teach and proclaim that fasting was a strategic offensive weapon to enhance prayer. I had used this passage to show that it was like bringing in the heavy artillery for prayer and intercession. I must tell you that part of what I had heard that morning from the Lord challenged this belief I held concerning fasting. I had made my case for my belief from this verse and the response that I heard in my spirit had completely caught me off guard. That shocking response was the reason to investigate this subject and share what I have had to relearn on it.

Early Translations and Surviving Manuscripts of the New Testament

When we look at the history of the New Testament and the various translations available to us, we owe a great debt of thanks to Johannes Gutenberg. He was the inventor of the printing press in 1440 AD, and it was his press that made possible the production of books and Bibles for the common person. The printing press made possible the widespread distribution of new thought and information, which the great reformers used in their day in the same way that bloggers use the internet today. The Luther Bible was printed in German in 1534; he had earlier translated and published the New Testament in 1522.

In England, another reformer William Tyndale would publish his translation of the New Testament in 1525. The publication of the Geneva Bible in 1560 became the most common translation in England, and it is said that 90% of this translation was influenced by the Tyndale Bible. The Geneva Bible was the one that the first pilgrims, the Puritans, brought to America. In 1611 the King James Bible was published, and it was deemed be the modern translation of its day. Over 50 scholars worked on this translation that drew from many of the already published translations, but its primary influence was clearly the Geneva Bible. These translations would have the greatest influences in future translations leading up to the modern age. Okay, so what has this got to do with Matthew 17:21?

What is so significant about all the history and the evolution of our modern New Testament is that it comes from one Greek translator's work; his name is Desiderius Erasmus. He was a Dutch Catholic scholar and priest who translated a version of the New Testament from the Greek texts in 1516 called, Textus Receptus. Previously, all of the Bibles that were translated into the languages of Europe came from the Latin texts used by the Catholic Church, such as the Latin Vulgate. This made his work the preferred source for the reformation era's translations throughout Western and Central Europe. From Martin Luther and William Tyndale to the Spanish Reina-Valera translation, the Russian Synod Bible, and the King James Version, they all heavily relied on the translation given by this noted Catholic scholar.

In the decades to follow, his work would be highly criticized and scrutinized for his liberality of interpretation. It is also the reason that many of the current modern translations use the oldest known manuscripts for their New Testament

Bibles. In them, you will find that they do not include Matthew 17:21 and more than 60 other nuances and additions from the Erasmus New Testament. The challenges he faced in his day in trying to stay true to his translation of the scriptures, is no different for the scholars of our day. It is very easy to reflect a current cultural paradigm and ideology into an ancient word from the Greek or Aramaic and form a thought that is not at its core meaning or interpretation.

Today's translators have a wealth of ancient manuscripts that may or may not have been available to translators like the scholar Erasmus. All ancient manuscripts can be carbon dated from the papyri and parchment to give us a chronological timeline. Some of these, like the Codex Sinaiticus, predate the Latin Vulgate Bible that was translated by Jerome in 382 AD. This work discovered in the Sinai Peninsula in 1844 was found with a completely undamaged New Testament, written on parchment.

Prior to this discovery, the Codex Vaticanus, which was dated around 300-325 AD was the unrivaled document of biblical antiquity. Documents such as these make up what is known today as the "Critical Text" that most new translations source for accuracy. It should be noted that both these ancient transcripts do not have the verse from Matthew 17:21. Today, many new translations are still produced and state that they are remaining true to the King James Version; they disclose this in their documentation.

So let's return to Mark's gospel and focus in on what was written:

> *"He replied, 'This kind can come out only by prayer'"* (Mark 9:29).

If you have spent any time in the study of the Bible you are no doubt familiar with three of the most common Greek words translated into English as "love," they would be *eros*, *phileo*, and *agape*. You may have even cracked open your concordance to look into the deeper meaning when that word "love" was used in a passage of Scripture. It is no different when investigating the word "prayer." It also has several Greek words that are simply translated as pray or prayer. In this passage from Mark, the Greek word *proseuche* is used and is one of the most difficult to articulate with one word into English. Look at the *Strong's Concordance* definition of the word "prayer" as used in Mark 9:29:

Strong's Concordance

proseuché: prayer

Original Word: προσευχή, ς,

Part of Speech: Noun, Feminine

Transliteration: *proseuché*

Phonetic Spelling: (pros-yoo-khay')

Short Definition: prayer, a place for prayer

Definition: (a) prayer (to God), (b) a place for prayer (used by Jews, perhaps where there was no synagogue).

The word *proseuche* conveys a picture of a place of prayer when there is no synagogue near. So what is the thought that this word is trying to convey? What does the picture of a synagogue convey to you, and how do you articulate it in a word or two? Remember when the gospels were written there were no formal churches at that time. There were house churches and outdoor meeting places. In some cases, they were permitted to gather at a synagogue where the Rabbi had a friendly disposition towards Christians. A synagogue would have conjured up the image of a place of worship, a place of reverence and an atmosphere or environment of prayer. In Acts 16:13, Paul goes by the river looking for a *proseuche;* this verse translates the thought as "a place of prayer":

> *"On the Sabbath day we went outside the city gate by the river, where we thought there was a place of prayer. We sat down and spoke to the women gathered there"* (Acts 16:13).

Now, picture a monk or a scholar in the early Middle Ages trying to make sense and give context to this Greek word from his paradigm of understanding. His viewpoint would be the church. That would convey to him a place of reverence and worship and an atmosphere of prayer. Furthermore, at this point of time in church history, fasting would be a symbol of piety and devotion to God. So you can see how a translator would find no difficulty relating those images into words as he translates this Greek word into English.

So then, how does one convey an atmosphere of prayer when there is no church in the vicinity? Another word, that is also simply translated and is the most common word to describe "pray or prayer" in the New Testament, is the Greek word *proseuchomai.* As you can see by the description below, it translates very simply and is a verb meaning that it is in action, whereas *proseuche* is a noun, which is a person, place or a thing.

> **Strong's Concordance**
>
> *proseuchomai*: to pray
>
> **Original Word:** προσεύχομαι
>
> **Part of Speech:** Verb
>
> **Transliteration:** *proseuchomai*
>
> **Phonetic Spelling:** (pros-yoo'-khom-ahee)
>
> **Short Definition:** I pray, pray for
>
> **Definition:** I pray, pray for, offer prayer.

How simple it would have been to explain the verse if the verb *proseuchomai* was used. Since that is not the word used here, let's reexamine what Jesus said privately to His disciples. If He had said that you need to pray using the common Greek word for prayer *proseuchomai*, how would that have been a revelation to the disciples?

In the midst of that chaotic scene on that morning, do you think that prayer never entered into the thoughts of the disciples? Furthermore, is any demon so great and powerful that it can stand up against the name of Jesus? And, is the name of Jesus not sufficient and powerful enough that it requires from you a prayer and fasting session? God forbid. At the very name of Jesus the demons tremble in terror before any Christian who believes in the all powerful and almighty name of the Lord!

Do you also think that Jesus would only now drop a truth bomb on them that would leave them unprepared to minister? Do you think He would say after the fact that fasting is necessary when neither He nor His disciples practiced fasting? Remember when the disciples of John the Baptist came asking Jesus why neither He nor His disciples fast? Jesus never denied that they were right in their assessment, so is He now changing course? You can see just by asking those questions that something is amiss. You can see how difficult the definition of a word like *proseuche* would be, and what a challenge it is to translate a word that carries a concept within it, and then try to assign a single word to it.

Jesus said, *"This kind can only come out by prayer."* So what would the verse look like if you incorporated the word *proseuche* as the noun that it is and use it in its described context? To convey its thought, you would have to use more than one word and it might read something like this:

"You need to maintain an environment of prayer when dealing with situations such as this."

Would this have been useful information for the disciples as they are learning how to move in the healing ministry? Are there any other examples in Scripture that show Jesus doing this and modeling it for His disciples? Here are just a few:

> *21When Jesus had again crossed over by boat to the other side of the lake, a large crowd gathered around him while he was by the lake. 22Then one of the synagogue leaders, named Jairus, came, and when he saw Jesus, he fell at his feet. 23He pleaded earnestly with him, "My little daughter is dying. Please come and put your hands on her so that she will be healed and live." 24So Jesus went with him.*
>
> *35While Jesus was still speaking, some people*

came from the house of Jairus, the synagogue leader. "Your daughter is dead," they said. "Why bother the teacher anymore?"

36Overhearing what they said, Jesus told him, "Don't be afraid; just believe."

37He did not let anyone follow him except Peter, James and John the brother of James. 38When they came to the home of the synagogue leader, Jesus saw a commotion, with people crying and wailing loudly. 39He went in and said to them, "Why all this commotion and wailing? The child is not dead but asleep." 40But they laughed at him. ***After he put them all out, he took the child's father and mother and the disciples who were with him, and went in where the child was.*** *41He took her by the hand and said to her, "Talitha koum!" (which means "Little girl, I say to you, get up!"). 42Immediately the girl stood up and began to walk around (she was twelve years old). At this they were completely astonished. 43He gave strict orders not to let anyone know about this, and told them to give her something to eat* (Mark 5:21-24a, 35-43).

In this wonderful account of the raising of Jairus' daughter from the dead, we see how Jesus changes the environment for prayer before He ministers to the child. He removed all of the people who mocked Him in unbelief concerning the girl, and He only allowed Peter, James, John and the parents to join Him in the room. Jesus changed the atmosphere for prayer by removing all of the unbelief from the room.

Here is another example of changing the environment or atmosphere for prayer:

> *22They came to Bethsaida, and some people brought a blind man and begged Jesus to touch him.* ***23He took the blind man by the hand and led him outside the village.*** *When he had spit on the man's eyes and put his hands on him, Jesus asked, "Do you see anything?"*
>
> *24He looked up and said, "I see people; they look like trees walking around."*
>
> *25Once more Jesus put his hands on the man's eyes. Then his eyes were opened, his sight was restored, and he saw everything clearly.* ***26Jesus sent him home, saying, "Don't even go into the village"*** (Mark 8:22-26).

A blind man is brought to Jesus who is asking for the healing touch of his hand. Jesus leads him out of the village of Bethsaida and heals him. He then gives him a curious instruction to not even go back into the village. Bethsaida was a notorious place of unbelief and Jesus said these words about it in Matthew 11:21, *"Woe to you, Chorazin! Woe to you, Bethsaida! For if the miracles that were performed in you had been performed in Tyre and Sidon, they would have repented long ago in sackcloth and ashes."* Once again, Jesus removes a person from an atmosphere of unbelief and changes the environment before ministering. Afterward, He did not even want the man to return to the village to be poisoned with their unbelief. This might have been a good example for the disciples to follow on that morning by taking that child aside to a private place for prayer.

Now let's take a look at another significant event when Jesus cleared the temple complex of what amounted to a marketplace bazaar:

> 12Jesus entered the temple courts and drove out all who were buying and selling there. He overturned the tables of the money changers and the benches of those selling doves. 13"It is written," he said to them, "'**My house will be called a house of prayer**,' but you are making it 'a den of robbers.'" **14The blind and the lame came to him at the temple, and he healed them.** 15But when the chief priests and the teachers of the law saw the wonderful things he did and the children shouting in the temple courts, "Hosanna to the Son of David," they were indignant.
>
> 16"Do you hear what these children are saying?" they asked him.
>
> "Yes," replied Jesus, "have you never read,
>
> "From the lips of children and infants
>
> you, Lord, have called forth your praise'?"
>
> 17And he left them and went out of the city to Bethany, where he spent the night (Matthew 21:12-17).

The religious leaders were profiting by allowing this marketplace to be set up on the temple grounds. Animals for the sacrificial offerings were being sold and temple treasury coins were being exchanged for offerings and the temple tax. Roman coins were not allowed in the treasury because of

Caesar's inscription on them. Therefore, the money exchange was required. It would also be safe to say other merchandise related to the Passover would also be on sale. The backdrop would have been a noisy scene of a numerous host of animals and throngs of people packed into the temple courts. Jesus drives them all out reminding them all that God's temple is a house of prayer.

Once again, the Greek word *proseuche* is used. Remember the definition of this word: a place of prayer in the absence of a synagogue. Of all the Greek words available that are translated into English as "prayer," this word is used. To suggest the absence of a synagogue when Jesus is referring to the temple, which is the mother of all synagogues, only further emphasizes the implied environment of prayer that is inherent in the use of that word. Look at how the whole scene plays out. The marketplace crowds are removed and the atmosphere of worship is restored as witnessed by the children shouting high praises to the Lord. And what is so beautiful to me is that we now see the blind, the lame, and the suffering come and receive their healing from the Lord of that house — Jesus, the Messiah.

Are you getting the picture? Well, let's see if the disciples understood this and practiced this later on as they ministered. From this next passage, we will see that Peter understood the principle and put it into practice.

> *36 In Joppa there was a disciple named Tabitha (in Greek her name is Dorcas); she was always doing good and helping the poor. 37About that time she became sick and died, and her body was washed and placed in an upstairs room. 38Lydda was near Joppa; so*

when the disciples heard that Peter was in Lydda, they sent two men to him and urged him, "Please come at once!"

39Peter went with them, and when he arrived he was taken upstairs to the room. All the widows stood around him, crying and showing him the robes and other clothing that Dorcas had made while she was still with them.

40Peter sent them all out of the room; then he got down on his knees and prayed. *Turning toward the dead woman, he said, "Tabitha, get up." She opened her eyes, and seeing Peter she sat up. 41He took her by the hand and helped her to her feet. Then he called for the believers, especially the widows, and presented her to them alive. 42This became known all over Joppa, and many people believed in the Lord. 43Peter stayed in Joppa for some time with a tanner named Simon* (Acts 9:36-43).

Here, we have a situation where a dear saint named Dorcas has just died. When they hear that Peter is nearby, they ask if he would come immediately; they hoped that God would do a miracle. Peter comes in response to their request, and he finds the women are in mourning and great sorrow. They show Peter the things that Dorcas made while she was alive and are undone by their loss of this dear saint. Peter's next course of action was to change the atmosphere for prayer. He sends them all out of the room and then prays for Dorcas, who is then raised from the dead.

Peter recognized that these precious women who so dearly

loved Dorcas were too overwhelmed by her passing. They were not in a place to rise up and take action with him in the prayer of faith. Peter was doing what he had seen Jesus model throughout his healing ministry. Oh, and by the way, the word translated as "prayed" in verse 40 is the verb, the action word, *proseuchomai*, the most common Greek word for prayer and engaging God.

It is from these conclusions that I agree with the modern translator's treatment of this passage when you look at the implied meaning of the Greek word used for prayer. It was from this study that my understanding was changed.

Lastly, what should have been a red flag for me is the fact that there were no other scriptures offering an agreement to the idea that fasting supercharges prayer. Here is another important rule of Bible study; when you see a "one off" and what I mean by that is, a scripture verse that has no other verses of Scriptures endorsing or agreeing with its implied use, it should make you pause. When I encounter a scripture verse like that, I quarantine it for a more detailed study. It may stand-alone, and it may not, but it is a good practice to adopt as you look deeper into the scriptures.

In summary, it was the unbelief surrounding the boy that hindered his healing. All three gospels recorded the event and agree that unbelief was the reason as stated by Jesus. Afterward, two of the gospels record the private discussion between Jesus and the disciples. From that conversation, a clear lesson was learned about ministering in an environment of unbelief. Even Jesus had difficulty ministering when He encountered this wall in the spirit of unbelief.

The Verse that Never Was

"He could not do any miracles there, except lay his hands on a few sick people and heal them. 6He was amazed at their lack of faith" (Mark 6:5).

Let's now read in this next chapter, what Jesus did teach on the subject of fasting.

Chapter 6

Fasting in the New Testament

It would be safe to say that the culture of fasting is firmly entrenched in Israel, especially after the post-Babylonian period. Faithful saints give themselves to prayer and fasting in honoring the religious traditions and many do it with sincere devotion to God. We see special mention being given by God to Anna, a prophet, who devoted herself to the Lord by praying day and night with fasting, hopefully awaiting Messiah's coming. God kept faithful Simeon and Anna alive to a late age in order to let them see Jesus the Promised One.

John the Baptist and his disciples would fast with such fervor that when they approached Jesus on the issue, they had put themselves on par with the Pharisees. The Sadducees and Pharisees were the new religious orders that were birthed in the exile, and they now shared religious governance in the nation. The Pharisees kept all the traditional fasts enacted as rites in Babylon and as a further practice, in addition to those days, they fasted twice a week. Saul of Tarsus would have most certainly been one of those who fervently kept the Law of Moses and the traditions of the elders as he was a devout Pharisee.

It is for these reasons that I have to ask why the subject of fasting is given very little attention in the New Testament? Why is there no instruction from Jesus, Peter or Paul in its use as an effective tool in spiritual warfare? Why do we see no corporate fasts by the early church or for that matter, even a call to fast? Why is it that in the midst of the persecutions that arose against the church from both the Jews and Gentiles from within the Roman Empire that we do not read of any fasting in response to the perils of their day? To me, the silence speaks volumes.

In this chapter, we will examine the scriptural references in the New Testament and discuss those scriptures that have not been written about thus far. We have discussed Jesus, and His one recorded fast. Now, we will move on to every other instance of fasting in the scriptures. I would also like to point out something that I find so important and lacking in the body of Christ today: the celebration of the Lord's Supper. Notice how the early church would come together as a body of believers.

> *"They devoted themselves to the apostles' teaching and to fellowship, to the breaking of bread and to prayer. 43Everyone was filled with awe at the many wonders and signs performed by the apostles"* (Acts 2:42, 43).

> *"Every day they devoted themselves to meeting together in the temple complex, and broke bread from house to house. They ate their food with a joyful and humble attitude, 47praising God and having favor with all the people. And every day the Lord added to them those who were being saved"* (Acts 2:46, 47).

When the believers came together, it was around the Word of God, prayer, and communion that led to a fellowship meal. Remember the definition of word "fast" from the Hebrew word *tsum;* it clearly states, "no food." If the early church is always celebrating the table of the Lord, they are violating their Jewish understanding of what a fast is in its description. In the New Testament, the words for "fast or fasting" are the Greek words *nesteuo* and *nesteia*, which literally mean, "to abstain from food and no food." There would have been no doubt in the minds of those early Jewish Christians as to what a fast meant in its practice. The partaking of communion would have been a violation of any fast day that a person was embarking upon.

Individual Fasts

The practice of individuals fasting in the New Testament is also a rare occurrence in the scriptural record. We see in the gospels that Anna the prophet fasted, John the Baptist fasted as did John's disciples. It should be noted that at this time, none of these people have crossed over into the New Covenant as Jesus had yet to go to the cross and rise from the dead in His glorification. John the Baptist is the last Old Covenant prophet, and the aforementioned people were awaiting Messiah's coming into His kingdom. Jesus would soon accommodate their heart's cry, but as of that reported time, they are all under the Law of Moses. The gospels record that the Pharisees fasted often. It is at this point, we will look further at Paul.

Paul

> 1Meanwhile, Saul was still breathing out murderous threats against the Lord's disciples. He went to the high priest 2and asked him for letters to the synagogues in Damascus, so that if he found any there who belonged to the Way, whether men or women, he might take them as

prisoners to Jerusalem. 3As he neared Damascus on his journey, suddenly a light from heaven flashed around him. 4He fell to the ground and heard a voice say to him, "Saul, Saul, why do you persecute me?"

5"Who are you, Lord?" Saul asked.

"I am Jesus, whom you are persecuting," he replied. 6"Now get up and go into the city, and you will be told what you must do."

7The men traveling with Saul stood there speechless; they heard the sound but did not see anyone. 8Saul got up from the ground, but when he opened his eyes he could see nothing. So they led him by the hand into Damascus. 9For three days he was blind, and did not eat or drink anything.

10In Damascus there was a disciple named Ananias. The Lord called to him in a vision, "Ananias!"

"Yes, Lord," he answered.

11The Lord told him, "Go to the house of Judas on Straight Street and ask for a man from Tarsus named Saul, for he is praying. 12In a vision he has seen a man named Ananias come and place his hands on him to restore his sight."

13"Lord," Ananias answered, "I have heard many reports about this man and all the harm he has done to your holy people in Jerusalem.

> *14And he has come here with authority from the chief priests to arrest all who call on your name."*
>
> *15But the Lord said to Ananias, "Go! This man is my chosen instrument to proclaim my name to the Gentiles and their kings and to the people of Israel. 16I will show him how much he must suffer for my name."*
>
> *17Then Ananias went to the house and entered it. Placing his hands on Saul, he said, "Brother Saul, the Lord—Jesus, who appeared to you on the road as you were coming here—has sent me so that you may see again and be filled with the Holy Spirit." 18Immediately, something like scales fell from Saul's eyes, and he could see again. He got up and was baptized, 19and after taking some food, he regained his strength* (Acts 9:1-18).

Up to this time, the man we know as the great apostle Paul is still the notorious Saul of Tarsus. It is through his passionate hatred of Christians that he is doing everything in his power to destroy this new faith in Jesus the Messiah. He has consented to deaths, forced Christians to recant their faith under severe beatings, pulled people from their homes and threw them into prison. If that isn't enough, he has now made plans to take his persecution outside of Israel and is on his way to Damascus with his band of bounty hunters. It is on that road that Saul will encounter Jesus and will be brought to Damascus as a blind man. This young, up and coming Pharisee who was trained under Gamaliel and who has made a great name for himself within the Sanhedrin for his persecution of Christians is now a blind man stranded in another country.

Now, to his horror, he learns that the very person he has hated the most is none other than God Almighty. This is not one of those conversion stories where the sky is bluer and the grass appears to be greener; he can't even see the brown sand under his feet. He has been party to murder against God's followers and committed horrible crimes against them; how sick inside he must have felt as he weighs in on his own actions. He will neither eat nor drink for three days. If Ananias had delayed his coming for another day, that could have spelled the end for Paul.

Some teach that Paul had entered into what is called an "Extreme Fast" as if he consciously purposed to do a fast unto the Lord. When you consider all of the circumstances surrounding him at that moment, do you really think that a purposeful fast was on his mind? I think that sitting in his blindness he would be feeling the full measure of condemnation and would be wondering what all the consequences of his actions will mean for him in the future. His life is now forever changed. It is no wonder that even years later, Paul would call himself the least of all the apostles.

The good news is that Paul will experience the gospel of grace in a measure that few can possibly know its depths. He will, with the same passion that drove him to evil, defend and proclaim the message of grace through faith to the world. He will also be virulent in its defense against those who want to bring any part of the new faith under the Law of Moses and those who preach that message will be met with curse and rebuke. The man named Saul is dead and the new man in

Christ Jesus will be from now on known as Paul.

Corporate Fasts

There will be so many monumental moments in the gospels and milestone events for the early church. Yet, they will be met without any reference to a fast that accompanied the event. We have no record in the gospels that the disciples of Jesus fasted, not even in preparation for the Day of Pentecost or during the heavy persecution that was led by Saul of Tarsus. What we do find are two occasions when the church leadership is seeking the Lord for wisdom and direction.

> 1Now in the church at Antioch there were prophets and teachers: Barnabas, Simeon called Niger, Lucius of Cyrene, Manaen (who had been brought up with Herod the tetrarch) and Saul. 2While they were worshiping the Lord and fasting, the Holy Spirit said, "Set apart for me Barnabas and Saul for the work to which I have called them." 3So after they had fasted and prayed, they placed their hands on them and sent them off (Acts 13:1-3).

The church of Jesus Christ is now entering its second decade, and it is only now that we see the first reference in Scripture of corporate fasting. What is clear from these two passages is that amongst the leadership, there was a perceived value in humbling themselves by fasting. In Antioch, we read that there were teachers and prophets, but this is about to be changed. Paul is still being called Saul, and he is named as being a part of those ministry gifts. Up to this point, he has not had one recorded demonstration of the power of the Holy Spirit in healing or miracles. What we do see from Paul at this time, is that he has been only ministering the Word in teaching and evangelism. It was after this fasting and prayer session that the Holy Spirit commissioned Paul and Barnabas as apostles. From this time forward, he will only be called Paul. You will see him move in his ministry with a new level of authority and manifest power.

> *"Paul and Barnabas appointed elders for them in each church and, with prayer and fasting, committed them to the Lord, in whom they had put their trust"* (Acts 14:23).

The second example we read is also with Paul and Barnabas. In every church that they will plant, they will appoint elders to care for each new body of believers. This was not taken lightly as with each new ordination, they would commit that new leadership to the Lord with prayer and fasting. These two examples, while being significant in Paul's ministry to the early church, are all that I can present to you as examples of corporate fasting in the New Testament. When you see fasting in relation to leadership appointments, it is surprising that the disciples of Jesus did not fast and pray for the replacement of Judas in appointing Matthias as the twelfth apostle. I can only point to the fact that Jesus did not model it to the disciples and that is why we do not see the practice of fasting by His disciples being recorded in the scriptures. We are now in the year 48 AD or 3808 on the Hebrew calendar.

There are no other offerings of personal examples of fasting that are left to discuss, so we will turn our attention to the teachings of Jesus on the subject.

Jesus on Fasting

Jesus will leave nothing off the table as He prepares His disciples and every future believer for their inheritance as saints and equipping them to carry on His ministry to the world. His life, His ministry, His works, His teachings and His heart are all for the purpose of bringing forth His royal priesthood in the earth. He has given the church all things that pertain to life and godliness. He has given us the Holy Spirit to dwell in us in order to manifest His authority and power in His name and to carry on the will of the Father on earth as it is in heaven. So, having said all that, why is there so little written in the New Testament regarding fasting? The following passages comprise the thoughts and teachings by Jesus on the subject.

> *16 "When you fast, do not look somber as the hypocrites do, for they disfigure their faces to show others they are fasting. Truly I tell you, they have received their reward in full. 17But when you fast, put oil on your head and wash your face, 18so that it will not be obvious to others that you are fasting, but only to your Father, who is unseen; and your Father, who sees what is done in secret, will reward you* (Matthew 6:16-18).

In the first passage, we see Jesus speaking to an audience that is well acquainted with the subject of fasting. The traditions and interpretive opinions by leading religious scholars throughout Israel's history have given them ritual days and the protocols for its practice. Jesus is not against fasting, but He does focus on what are your reasons for doing it.

The Pharisees will make a good show to everyone they are upholding their piety before all to see, which is completely contrary to an act of contrition and humbling oneself before God. This is nothing more than an act of shameless pride, which carries a promise that God will resist those who flaunt pride before Him. Those things that are truly done unto the Lord are done in secret, not for the praise of man. These acts are known only to God; He is your audience of one from whom you seek to receive praise.

In this next passage from Luke's gospel we read:

> *33They said to him, "John's disciples often fast and pray, and so do the disciples of the Pharisees, but yours go on eating and drinking."*
>
> *34Jesus answered, "Can you make the friends of the bridegroom fast while he is with them? 35But the time will come when the bridegroom will be taken from them; in those days they will fast."*
>
> *36He told them this parable: "No one tears a piece out of a new garment to patch an old one. Otherwise, they will have torn the new garment, and the patch from the new will not match the old. 37And no one pours new wine into old wineskins. Otherwise, the new wine will burst the skins; the wine will run out and the wineskins will be ruined. 38No, new wine must be poured into new wineskins. 39And no one after drinking old wine wants the new, for they say, 'The old is* better" (Luke 5:33-39).

The disciples of John have come to Jesus obviously troubled over the lack of piety shown by Him and His disciples. John's disciples and the Pharisees fast often in self-abasement and denial, while Jesus and His disciples seem to be always feasting. I can't help but think that John the Baptist approved of their query because he has spent his entire life as one who has been given to a sacrificial lifestyle, wholly dedicated to the observance of the Law of Moses.

You will notice that Jesus neither denies what they are saying is true nor corrects them by acknowledging that they do, in fact, practice fasting. Instead, He tells them that this is a celebration because a wedding is about to take place and that is why fasting is inappropriate at this time. The picture that the Lord is painting is that He is the bridegroom celebrating with His disciples who are the bridal party waiting for the moment when His glorious and beautiful bride (you, the church) will be revealed. For all that our Lord endured in His ministry and all that He suffered at the cross, nothing could steal His joy of becoming one with you – His bride.

Jesus then goes on and tells them that when the bridegroom is taken away from the disciples that *"in those days they will fast."* So when will those days be? In John 16, Jesus speaks of His departure and the scripture records that upon hearing these words, the disciples' hearts were filled with sorrow. He then goes on to say:

> *19Jesus saw that they wanted to ask him about this, so he said to them, "Are you asking one another what I meant when I said, 'In a little while you will see me no more, and then after a little while you will see me'? 20Very truly I tell you, you will weep and mourn while the world*

> rejoices. You will grieve, but your grief will turn to joy. 21A woman giving birth to a child has pain because her time has come; but when her baby is born she forgets the anguish because of her joy that a child is born into the world. 22So with you: Now is your time of grief, but I will see you again and you will rejoice, and no one will take away your joy. 23In that day you will no longer ask me anything. Very truly I tell you, my Father will give you whatever you ask in my name. 24Until now you have not asked for anything in my name. Ask and you will receive, and your joy will be complete (John 16:19-24).

Jesus is speaking very clearly about the time when He, the bridegroom, will be taken away and that through the promised Holy Spirit, He will always be with them. Their short period of grieving and mourning will be turned again to great joy. If the Lord was inferring that His ascension would mean the commencement of fasting, then the gospel should not be called the Good News; it should be called the sorrowful news. Instead, their time of sorrow would be a very short one.

The promise of our joy being complete is because of the precious gift of the Holy Spirit who dwells in the heart of every believer. Jesus modeled for us a life complete in the Father and the disciples walked out His example for us in the scriptures. That is why we have no teachings in the epistles in relation to the practice of fasting in the early church for Jewish gatherings of believers or the Gentile churches.

Returning to Luke Chapter 5, we see that the conversation

Jesus is having with the disciples of John does not end at verse 35. He gives them two parables to reveal that things are about to be radically changed and that a new normal is coming. The Lord speaks of a new cloth and an old garment. In the second parable, He speaks of a new wine and a new wineskin.

Remember, as we have said before, the context is the key to seeing the unfolding of a scriptural passage. The context is about Jesus' lack of following the traditions of their religion as set down by the elders. The focus of the context is fasting and Jesus answers the question and gives illustrations of the changes that are coming. These changes will be so dramatic that it will be impossible to keep the status quo. To do so will cause greater damage to the old garment and destruction to the old wineskin.

Jesus said that He did not come to destroy the law and the prophets, He came to fulfill them. The Law of Moses is the old garment and is in need of repair. The righteousness that it provides cannot hide mankind's nakedness. To try to place a patch taken from the new garment of which the Holy Spirit is interwoven into the thread of this garment will prove to be incompatible. A new piece of the unshrunk cloth from this new garment will only worsen the tear on that already damaged garment.

The New Covenant is that new garment given as a gift of grace by Jesus and offered freely to all mankind. It is the robe of righteousness that is found only in Christ and received by grace through faith. It is the very nature of Christ Jesus that is woven into every aspect of the fabric of this new garment. In Exodus 39, we read that the priestly garments, particularly, the Ephod had gold interwoven into the fabric. Gold symbolizes purity, royalty, and wealth. The Holy Spirit is the invisible thread that characterizes the nature of God that we are privileged to adorn ourselves with and cover our nakedness. The Law of Moses, as symbolized by the old garment, cannot be repaired by the new cloth; it has served its purpose and has to be replaced.

Likewise, the old wineskin, which is the Old Covenant, has been stretched to its maximum capacity. To add new wine, which is representative of the Holy Spirit and its living, fermenting activities, will only burst the old wineskin, making it unusable. This new wine, in this new wineskin, will in time make for a vintage so masterfully aged, so full bodied, that once tasted, the world will see that it has no equal.

The vintage year is now more than two thousand years old and a fully-aged wine is a preferred choice. Jesus was telling all who could hear, that the way they perceived the things of God and understood them, will all be changed. What Jesus will usher in, will forever change the world and their understanding of God and His ways.

In keeping with the context, which is fasting, how will it be changed in the New Covenant? Jesus had said the monumental shift is coming, so we wait and with listening ears, we search the book of Acts, the Epistles and on through to the book of Revelation for that powerful revelation. Instead, we are presented with silence on the subject, and all we hear are the sounds of crickets.

If the scriptures are silent in the New Covenant, then God's heart on the matter must be hidden in the shadows of the Old Covenant. If it is found in the shadows, then it cannot be from the Law of Moses; it must then be found in the prophets. Isaiah has much to say on this subject and his prophetic word still has not resounded from the rooftops loud enough to penetrate our ears. Let's look into the prophetic word that has been lying dormant throughout the ages.

Chapter 7

The Fast that I Have Chosen

Isaiah 58

I have often used the phrase "the silence of God is deafening" especially when I am trying to engage the mind of Christ, and I am not hearing His voice clearly. What I have found is that when I have uttered those words, it is more often than not, that God is speaking, but I am not hearing. So often, it is my understanding of things that are like colored lenses of my own beliefs that keep me from seeing the clear picture. As it relates to my ears, these beliefs work like earplugs, which hinder my ability to hear.

I cannot tell you how many times over the course of my life that I have read Isaiah's 58th chapter and completely missed its message. I see the word "fast," and I immediately enter a concept and understanding of the subject of fasting. I read this passage through the lens of that paradigm and miss the entire message of what God is saying in it. I must confess that I am not alone in this; I have read other authors on this subject who have addressed this chapter in the exact same way as I once did. God is speaking about the type of fast that He has chosen for His people, and He never asks you to even miss a single meal.

So many faithful leaders and intercessors look to fasting as a major catalyst to their prayer life. They are tireless in their labor to see the kingdom of God manifest itself in power and see the Lord rescue and change their communities. I would ask that as you read this chapter that you remain open to what God is asking of His people and what He is promising. Then, receive what He has said and enter into His Sabbath rest.

When I think back to that morning when I heard these words, "You have fasted unto me when you have broken the fast of others," I had no idea that God was going to turn my whole understanding of fasting upside down. That study led me to Jesus' words of a new wineskin for the new wine that was coming, and fasting was the context of the subject matter.

The New Covenant will function and operate in ways previously unfamiliar to how we as people would have done things in the past. Just as the entire plan of salvation in the New Covenant was hidden within the Old Covenant, God's heart concerning the subject of fasting was laying dormant in the prophetic words of Isaiah and Zechariah.

God, through the prophet Zechariah, proclaimed to Israel that He wanted to change their fast days to feast days; He was speaking of a new way of thinking. But nowhere is it more clearly stated as to what is in God's heart concerning fasting, than what we read in Isaiah 58:

> *1"Shout it aloud, do not hold back. Raise your voice like a trumpet. Declare to my people their rebellion and to the descendants of Jacob their sins. 2For day after day they seek me out; they seem eager to know my ways, as if they were a nation that does what is right and has not forsaken the commands of its God. They ask me*

> *for just decisions*
>
> *and seem eager for God to come near them. 3'Why have we fasted,' they say, 'and you have not seen it? Why have we humbled ourselves, and you have not noticed?' "Yet on the day of your fasting, you do as you please and exploit all your workers. 4Your fasting ends in quarreling and strife, and in striking each other with wicked fists. You cannot fast as you do today and expect your voice to be heard on high. 5 Is this the kind of fast I have chosen, only a day for people to humble themselves? Is it only for bowing one's head like a reed and for lying in sackcloth and ashes? Is that what you call a fast, a day acceptable to the Lord? 6"Is not this the kind of fasting I have chosen: to loose the chains of injustice and untie the cords of the yoke, to set the oppressed free and break every yoke? 7Is it not to share your food with the hungry and to provide the poor wanderer with shelter—when you see the naked, to clothe them, and not to turn away from your own flesh and blood?*

Wow! Israel, on the surface, seems to be doing all the right things and is giving the appearance they have all the right motives for conducting a fast. They are seeking to know God's will and looking for His justice by drawing near to God. They have humbled themselves with fasting to show God that they are sincere in their prayer and petitions. They go all out putting on sackcloth, covering themselves with ashes. They are bowing down and lying prostrate on the floor only to be exasperated in the fact that God does not seem to notice or care. It is as if God is saying "You are putting on a good show, but I'm not buying it." God is completely indifferent to their outward expressions of piety and contrition because He sees what is really at work in their hearts.

The Lord points to their conduct and exposes their abuses against one another in strife and violent acts, which reveal a degree of hatred for their fellow man. He asks them if they really think that these outward shows of not eating and other outward shows of humility, is the kind of fasting that will draw the attention of God? The prophetic word is indicting Israel's fasting as merely a self-righteous work to manipulate God into action, for their own purposes. God then poses the question back to them by essentially saying, "Do you really think that this kind of fasting is acceptable to me?" All this effort to get God's focus and attention to their needs and wants are met with complete indifference to their outward displays of piety.

The Lord then challenges the nation to a completely different course of action. Instead of yoking yourselves with affliction in sackcloth and ashes, break the yoke of the affliction on behalf of others who cannot deliver themselves. Come to the aid of their injustices and set them free. Instead of denying yourself by fasting, give meals to the hungry and help them with shelter, clothing, and their most basic needs. It can be very easy to spiritualize this passage and ignore the true context of this prophetic word and the social responsibility that goes with it.

Those of us who live in the West deem this to be our governments' responsibility with the church adding its charity when it feels led to do so. We think that we can offer fasting and spiritual warfare with prayer in the place of the ministry to the poor and afflicted. If we are being honest with ourselves, we consider this a low-level service within our churches and ministries. Yet, this was one of the two keys to the explosive growth of the early church within the Roman Empire. The move of God is what you are crying out for but the spiritual harvest of promise is seeded by the practical ministry of love.

The Conqueror Conquers the Conquerors

When you listen to any great sermon about the early church and its growth throughout the world, you will hear about the extreme sacrifices of the saints and what led to their martyrdom for the faith. As a young man hearing these messages, I would be stirred in my heart that I too would be willing to lay my life down for the cause of Christ. It was in their death and how they died that caused the world to marvel about this new faith. It stirred up an interest in them to know more about this Jesus for whom they would die so well. It is definitely true that when the church endures persecution, the body of Christ expands and grows as a result of its endured trials.

These are those bright and shining moments of glory, but moments they are when you consider the overall span of time. What about the everyday role of the church in its ministry to a completely pagan Roman world? Before the great periods of persecution that the church endured, Christianity was a mystery religion. The Romans had no concept of what they were seeing and hearing about this new group, only understanding it to be some absurd form of the Jewish religion. Yet, it would grow rapidly.

To better understand this, I went to source materials that were not Christian but, in fact, were from pagan Romans writings to see through their eyes what they thought of this new illegal religion. What you find from these early writings and more detailed accounts from Pliny the Younger, Celsus and other less notable names are often horrific accounts of what they believed were the practices of these Christians. The things they had heard about concerning what went on in their secret meetings would be shocking to even the most debaucherous Roman. They describe secret rites of cannibalism, whereby, human flesh is eaten and human blood is consumed. Therefore, presuming murder and human sacrifice, I think you know what this is referring to. Imagine if a Roman citizen who overhears someone quoting the words of Jesus from His last Passover meal as they partake of communion together. What would that person be thinking? There are so many other documented reports that are equally hideous about Christians that it would make one wonder how the church was growing at all?

What we do learn from the confused Roman reports was that they assumed that Christians were part of an association or organization of sorts. One writer claims that the Christian group is "a burial society," another, "like that of a fireman's society" or like "a trade association assuming that fees for joining are the reason for the benefits that are provided." What is clear to these Romans is that these Christians whoever they were, are providing a benefit to their community.

In the Roman world of the first and second century, charity among its citizenry was not the norm. The rich would give gifts to the poor as a show of benevolence for their own personal glorification and praise. The government knew that if the people had bread, that the peace would be kept, and order would be maintained. The emperors knew that by offering the people free entertainment at the coliseums it would make for a good distraction from the real lives of the common people. If you were poor or suffering, it was your fate from the gods, and you had little recourse to fight against it.

Into this world comes the church of Jesus Christ; the world begins to taste and see the love of God in action. Over 2300 years ago, Plato described love in this way, "Love is the movement of man toward ever higher things." Socrates asks the question: "Must not love be only love of beauty and not ugliness?" He also goes on to say, "Love ever dwells with want." The roots of our western culture, philosophy, democracy, and thought come to us from the ancient Greeks. Their commonly used word for love, *eros* meant something to possess and pursue to the highest, the best, and most beautiful. That kind of love is never satisfied and when it no longer receives its adequate gratification, it begins to look for something else deemed to be better, higher or more beautiful.

The New Testament, also written in ancient Greek, purposely ignores and omits the common word used for love in its day. Instead, a seldom-used word *agape* became their definition of love. The world was reaching for higher, better and more beautiful, rejecting everything and everyone that would fall short of that ideal. The church began reaching out to all that their society and culture saw as not worthy of its love. The church was thought to be a burial society because of the dignity it gave to its dead by giving them a proper burial and funeral no matter what the person's status was in life.

The city of Rome's population was more than a million people at that time. It would have been comprised of a slave population that would have made up about a third of that total. A mere slave on his or her death would be simply thrown out at the dump or tossed into the river. The early church offered them community and gave these people love and value in Christ. The Good News began to flourish among the slaves freeing them in a way the pagans could not understand. The Roman soldiers lived hard lives and were mostly comprised from the vassal states of the empire; they were promised citizenship for time served. The Christian communities were reaching the lower ranks through the gospel and the care for their families. This also proved true for the poor throughout the empire. They witnessed the demonstration of the Spirit and power of God and experienced the daily display of the *agape* of God in the most practical terms.

The church of God was experiencing rapid growth amongst the poor and disenfranchised people of the empire. Paul wrote in his letter to the Corinthians:

> *26Brothers and sisters, think of what you were when you were called. Not many of you were wise by human standards; not many were influential; not many were of noble birth. 27But God chose the foolish things of the world to shame the wise; God chose the weak things of the world to shame the strong. 28God chose the lowly things of this world and the despised things—and the things that are not—to nullify the things that are, 29so that no one may boast before him* (1 Corinthians 1:26-29).

Pliny the Younger would report to Emperor Trajan that complaints are rising in certain cities against the Christians from some of the trades experiencing a loss of business to those industries that cater to the local temples. Idol makers, smiths, and even butchers that sold the excess meat from the daily offerings were seeing a decline in demand for their goods and services. The day-to-day manifestation of the love of God was being shown in the most practical ways and was systematically disarming the pagan Empire and the spiritual principalities that ruled over it.

There is a perception in some parts of the body of Christ that we are still living in a time similar to Daniel's day whereby spiritual principalities and powers rule in the heavenly places over regions. This not entirely the case because Jesus defeated all power and rule and returned it to mankind through Christ. Ruling spirits and powers only have authority to operate their rogue principalities and rule when they are given that right by the people of that city, region, state or country. Those communities exchange their freedom for the enslavement of sin that those principalities and powers offer in order to regain a degree of rule. That is why a particular region or city may be known for its crime, vice or even religion.

> *13When you were dead in your sins and in the uncircumcision of your flesh, God made you alive with Christ. He forgave us all our sins, 14having canceled the charge of our legal indebtedness, which stood against us and condemned us; he has taken it away, nailing it to the cross. 15And having disarmed the powers and authorities, he made a public spectacle of them, triumphing over them by the cross* (Colossians. 2:13-15).

Jesus completely conquered the powers of darkness and disarmed them in their defeat. But, it is the people who will choose who they want to serve, empower, and become their ruler. If a community chooses to give itself to a particular sin, they are giving those defeated spirits the right and power to rule. We the church want to disarm and dethrone these rogue demonic principalities. We think the strategy is to fire the arrows of intercession in warfare against them, to topple their rogue rule. But what we fail to see is that those demonic powers are shielded by the people who have chosen them to rule over them by deception or by choice. Those people have become human shields protecting Satan's right to remain in power. Evangelism in all its forms proclaiming the Good News, removes each human shield, one believing person at a time until that demonic power is weakened to the point that it has no right to the seat of authority over a city.

The warfare of Jesus is exhibited through His ministry, fulfilling the Isaiah 61 mandate of the Messiah. Every believer is commissioned to carry this same work forward in the earth, continuing it in Jesus' name and for His glory. When the intercession ministry and evangelism ministry in all its forms work together in a city or region, the results will mirror those of the early church. The expression of the love of God through those churches and the fact that they loved not their lives even unto death overwhelmed the culture and beliefs of pagan Rome and its Empire.

So, in returning to Isaiah 58, we see in it the promises of God that all faithful prayer warriors are seeking for their communities and the body of Christ. God is promising that if His people would take on the cause of the poor and afflicted, then He will move in mighty power on behalf of His people. A practical work unleashes a spiritual release of the power and glory of God. Isaiah's prophetic word goes on to say,

> *"Then your light will break forth like the dawn, and your healing will quickly appear; then your righteousness will go before you, and the glory of the Lord will be your rear guard. 9Then you will call, and the Lord will answer; you will cry for help, and he will say: Here am I" (Isaiah 58:8, 9).*

God promises to those who may seem hidden as if in the night that they will find that their light will break forth like the dawn. Think about that verse for a moment, you may be in a country that has no regard for Jesus or it may be just your city and region. It could be that your work seems hidden, even your own ministry is seemingly hidden away with little voice to your community or even your own church. The Lord is promising His people that if we attend to His desire, He will cause a breaking forth of His glory to emerge on our behalf and expel whatever the darkness may have been.

Furthermore, healing will quickly appear for His people and, of course, to set free the oppressed. So often we are claiming, declaring and believing for the manifestation of the healing anointing, yet, there seems to be a disconnect somewhere. In this passage, God declares it with a promise that the Lord Jesus who is our righteousness will go before us, paving the way in advance and also protecting us from behind. He will lead the way into battle and be your rearguard, you will be enveloped in His protection and care. No longer waiting or suffering in silence because when you call His name, He will answer you speedily. This promise is already a cup that is running over, but there's more:

> *If you do away with the yoke of oppression, with the pointing finger and malicious talk, 10and if you spend yourselves in behalf of the hungry and satisfy the needs of the oppressed, then your light will rise in the darkness, and your night will become like the noonday. 11The Lord will guide you always; he will satisfy your needs in a sun-scorched land and will strengthen your frame. You will be like a well-watered garden,*
>
> *like a spring whose waters never fail. 12Your people will rebuild the ancient ruins and will raise up the age-old foundations; you will be called Repairer of Broken Walls, Restorer of Streets with Dwellings (Isaiah 58: 10-12).*

If we no longer speak evil of one another out of spite or envy and put away from us the critical and judging spirit. If we walk in love to those in our cities or among those that are different from us and serve those less fortunate, the morning sun that greeted us earlier now becomes the noonday sun in all its strength. Now, we move from a little bit of light to the manifestation of our God in all His glory. No more groping in the darkness seeking for God's direction, but now seeing His guidance in the brightest of days. No matter how intense that sun may seem to all who are around you, you live with the promise that your crops, your work in the Lord will be like a well-watered garden. You will have wellsprings of the Spirit of God creating pools of blessings that will never run dry. God will unstop the ancient wells in your cities, awaken the destiny and restore those mantles and callings.

The Lord will place upon you that honor of recognition of

your faithfulness to be a co-laborer together with Christ in His works. People will see that the mantle of the restorer is on you, as one who rebuilds and brings healing to individuals, churches, cities, and even nations. These promises seem so overwhelming that they should be given to us for simply demonstrating His heart for the oppressed. We should be doing all of these even if there was no promise of these blessings being offered by God. To allow the love of God to flow through us is one of the highest privileges we have as believers. Yet, having said all of this, the promise of blessings do not end here; there is still more:

> *13If you keep your feet from breaking the Sabbath and from doing as you please on my holy day, if you call the Sabbath a delight and the Lord's holy day honorable, and if you honor it by not going your own way and not doing as you please or speaking idle words, 14then you will find your joy in the Lord, and I will cause you to ride in triumph on the heights of the land and to feast on the inheritance of your father Jacob." The mouth of the Lord has spoken (Isaiah 58:13, 14).*

There is something so powerful in the message of the Sabbath rest because it is a conscious action of ceasing from your own labor. In the New Covenant, Jesus is our Sabbath rest; it is in Him that we find our peace and rest. It is no longer just one day a week of rest, but the promised rest is now every day, in Him. So to be in Christ and dwell in that reality by faith and anchoring our hearts and minds in Him, we are promised a joy that will take us to victorious heights in the kingdom of God.

You probably have confirmed as you have read through this chapter, that there is not one reference to anyone being asked to fast or miss a meal in Isaiah's prophecy. The type of fast that God has chosen in this prophecy ends with a feast, a banquet of all that our inheritance in Christ has provided us. God is awesome! If there should be anyone who may doubt what Isaiah has prophesied, he ends the word with, *"The mouth of the Lord has spoken."*

Early Church Writings on this Subject

Since there is no private interpretation given as it relates to Scripture, I thought it best to search through the early church writings on the subject to see if there is any agreement on this premise that Isaiah 58 is the New Covenant model for fasting. I also wanted to make sure that if I put something forward from non-biblical works that the teacher or his writings were accepted by the early church. What I found very striking was the Epistle of Barnabas that was probably written before 100 AD. His work has been cited and written of by the early apostolic fathers, such as Origin and Clement of Alexandria; this gave me confidence in quoting his writings on fasting.

So, is this writer the Barnabas from the book of Acts? I cannot say, but it certainly has some strong defense against returning in any way to the Law of Moses, which has the same earmarks of Paul's writings. I should also point out that the Epistle of Barnabas should not be confused with the fake Gospel of Barnabas, which was an early Middle Ages Islamic propaganda work to discredit the deity of Jesus. Also, another question may be asked, how should we view a study from an early non-biblical work? Reading the Epistle of Barnabas would be no different than reading something from any Christian author, except for the fact that it is probably one of the oldest early church documents that is not a part of the scriptures, as it was rediscovered much later on in time. Here is what Barnabas had to say about fasting:

CHAPTER III.--THE FASTS OF THE JEWS ARE NOT TRUE FASTS, NOR ACCEPTABLE TO GOD.

He says then to them again concerning these things:

> Why do ye fast to Me as on this day, saith the Lord, that your voice should be heard with a cry? I have not chosen this fast, saith the Lord, that a man should humble his soul. Nor, though ye bend your neck like a ring, and put upon you sackcloth and ashes, will ye call it an acceptable fast." To us He saith, "Behold, this is the fast that I have chosen, saith the Lord, not that a man should humble his soul, but that he should loose every band of iniquity, untie the fastenings of harsh agreements, restore to liberty them that are bruised, tear in pieces every unjust engagement, feed the hungry with thy bread, clothe the naked when thou seest him, bring the homeless into thy house, not despise the humble if thou behold him, and not [turn away] from the members of thine own family. Then shall thy dawn break forth, and thy healing shall quickly spring up, and righteousness shall go forth before thee, and the glory of God shall encompass thee; and then thou shalt call, and God shall hear thee; whilst thou art yet speaking, He shall say,

Behold, I am with thee; if thou take away from thee the chain [binding others], and the stretching forth of the hands [to swear falsely], and words of murmuring, and give cheerfully thy bread to the hungry, and show compassion to the soul that has been humbled." To this end, therefore, brethren, He is long-suffering, foreseeing how the people whom He has prepared shall with guilelessness believe in His Beloved. For He revealed all these things to us beforehand, that we should not rush forward as rash acceptors of their laws.

As you have just read, in this letter from Barnabas, he quotes the same passage from Isaiah 58 and is essentially saying the same thing that I have put forward in this chapter.

God gives through Isaiah's prophetic word the action plan of His heart and care and His desire to bless His people radically when they join in His labor of love. So how then do we model this out in the current day? What is the action plan that can bring the results that the early church witnessed? God has given a practical word that transitions into spiritual results and then manifests itself again into the natural realm. This is the template we must follow to see the promised result.

Chapter 8

Walking It Out

Hitting the Reset Button

I believe the body of Christ needs to reclaim the Isaiah 58 mantle of ministry. The testimony of the early church in the Judean and Gentile churches is that they cared for their own. This sent a powerful message to the unsaved within the Roman Empire that the church of Jesus Christ lives what it believes. It was not mere lip service saying, "be warm and be filled brother" but it was one of action. With the community strong, their voices to the unsaved grew stronger in word and deed. If we solely leave this responsibility to the government, we will see our voices to the poor and disenfranchised in our communities continue to weaken. If we take up this mantle and administer it within the Isaiah 61 mandate of the Lord, I believe a great move of God can take hold of our cities.

I have written on the prophecy and promises from Isaiah 58 in the previous chapter, so I should now explain what I mean by the Isaiah 61 mandate:

> *1The Spirit of the Sovereign Lord is on me, because the Lord has anointed me to proclaim good news to the poor. He has sent me to bind up the brokenhearted, to proclaim freedom for*

> the captives and release from darkness for the prisoners, 2to proclaim the year of the Lord's favor (Isaiah 61:1).

Jesus quoted this passage in His first public message after He had returned from His 40-day fast in the wilderness. He stopped part way through the second verse and then rolled up the scroll telling them that the scripture has now come to pass before their very eyes. Every devout Jew knew that this passage spoke of the Messiah and described His works. How often did the Pharisees and Sadducees ask for proof that Jesus was the Messiah? How often would Jesus reply that His works testify of who He is? The first objective of Messiah's ministry was to the poor with a proclamation of Good News. This would be true for any person, whether poor spiritually or poor materially. So how does telling a person that is already beaten down by life "Repent for the kingdom of God is here" help? How does that offer hope and help to the poor?

Christianity at large has taken the same viewpoint that a Jewish person under the Law of Moses would have had. You are under judgment for all your sins, and you had better repent or it's going to get worse for you. That's how the word "repent" was viewed under the Law of Moses. You see that inference and understanding being used right up to the last prophet of the Old Testament — John the Baptist. When you see John's call to repent and contrast it to Jesus and His call to repent, you see a stark and major contrast; it is, in fact, a major paradigm shift. Let's compare the two,

> In those days John the Baptist came, preaching in the wilderness of Judea 2and saying, "Repent, for the kingdom of heaven has come near." 3This is he who was spoken of through

the prophet Isaiah: "A voice of one calling in the wilderness, 'Prepare the way for the Lord, make straight paths for him.' 4John's clothes were made of camel's hair, and he had a leather belt around his waist. His food was locusts and wild honey. 5People went out to him from Jerusalem and all Judea and the whole region of the Jordan. 6Confessing their sins, they were baptized by him in the Jordan River.

7But when he saw many of the Pharisees and Sadducees coming to where he was baptizing, he said to them: "You brood of vipers! Who warned you to flee from the coming wrath? 8Produce fruit in keeping with repentance. 9And do not think you can say to yourselves, 'We have Abraham as our father.' I tell you that out of these stones God can raise up children for Abraham. 10The ax is already at the root of the trees, and every tree that does not produce good fruit will be cut down and thrown into the fire. 11"I baptize you with water for repentance. But after me comes one who is more powerful than I, whose sandals I am not worthy to carry. He will baptize you with the Holy Spirit and fire. 12His winnowing fork is in his hand, and he will clear his threshing floor, gathering his wheat into the barn and burning up the chaff with unquenchable fire" (Matthew 3:1-12).

This is the message of repentance through the lens of the Law of Moses, which was still the covenant in place during John the Baptist's ministry. Luke's gospel records that John said this to the crowds, not just the Pharisees and Sadducees. Now, if life had beaten you down to poverty, whether spiritually, naturally or both, how does one more condemning word that probably already plays out in your mind every day anyway, become good news?

Now let's look at Jesus conveying the same message,

> *"After John was put in prison, Jesus went into Galilee, proclaiming the good news of God. 15 'The time has come,' he said. 'The kingdom of God has come near. Repent and believe the good news!'"* (Mark 1:14, 15).

> *"From that time on Jesus began to preach, 'Repent, for the kingdom of heaven has come near'"* (Matthew 4:17).

Herod the Tetrarch has thrown John the Baptist into prison for speaking against his marriage to Herodias, his brother's wife. It will be from that time forward that Jesus will continue the proclamation of John but in a completely different way. Jesus is proclaiming the same initial words, but with a different message. He is telling people to repent and believe the good news about God. The Greek word used in these passages for "repent" is an action word, *metanoeó*, which means to change your mind with intent or purpose. So what's so good about that news?

> **Strong's Concordance**
>
> *metanoeó*: to change one's mind or purpose
>
> **Original Word:** μετανοέω
>
> **Part of Speech:** Verb
>
> **Transliteration:** *metanoeó*
>
> **Phonetic Spelling:** (met-an-o-eh'-o)
>
> **Short Definition:** I repent, change my mind
>
> **Definition:** I repent, change my mind, change the inner man (particularly with reference to acceptance of the will of God), repent.

What Jesus was telling Israel was change your mind about God and your belief about how God feels towards you. Change your mind that God is hostile towards you. Change your belief about God because it's not a day of judgment. Rather, it is a year of His favor. I think it is with a purpose that Jesus rolls up the scroll after reading only half of verse two. He does that in order to prevent any confusion about His message to Israel.

The message Jesus was proclaiming was healing, deliverance, freedom, and an environment of favor so great upon you that days and months cannot diminish it. That was the Messiah mandate of our Lord Jesus. If you have any doubts that He is not speaking to you today in the same way, you need to repent and change your mind about God. It does not stop there because His mandate is our mandate, which is the Great Commission to proclaim Jesus as the Christ of God and this same message of grace and favor. Add the demonstration of the power of the Holy Spirit, and you will now have the picture of the early church in action.

When Jesus completed delivering what might have been one of the shortest sermons of all time, He went out and put the word immediately into practice,

> *23Jesus went throughout Galilee, teaching in their synagogues, proclaiming the good news of the kingdom, and healing every disease and sickness among the people. 24News about him spread all over Syria, and people brought to him all who were ill with various diseases, those suffering severe pain, the demon-possessed, those having seizures, and the paralyzed; and he healed them. 25Large crowds from Galilee, the Decapolis, Jerusalem, Judea and the region across the Jordan followed him* (Matthew 4:23-25).

Did you notice that the ministry to the poor in Isaiah 58 brings forth a release of the healing anointing? You didn't even have to miss a meal to get it, because it comes by virtue of His promise to you, as you give your bread to the hungry. I am not promising you this, God is. When you touch matters close to His heart, He will most assuredly touch the matters close to yours.

If we look back at the early church and seek to adopt the heart of the Isaiah 58 message, it may require a dramatic shift from our Western world thinking. It was no coincidence that in times of plague and famine, the church grew even while the overall population was decreasing in those times of great distress. During times of plague, the Christians set up what may have been the first type of hospital care for their own, and they also refused no one who came to them for help. In times of famine, we see in the book of Acts that the body of Christ reaches out beyond its own cities to offer help and aid wherever it is needed. Is this true of the body of Christ today? Of course, it is, but what is done by the few, should be the mandate of the many.

Today, the government is looked to as the people's source for wellbeing and safety. This carries within it a level of truth that has been in existence since communities and nations were formed. But, the more active a government becomes in the lives of its citizenry, greater is its expectation of its influence in your life. The reality is that it could be a good thing, but it could also be a bad thing; that is dependent on who is in power.

We have seen a dramatic shift in the West over the last two generations that has instilled a humanistic culture that has gradually increased the resistance to its Christian heritage. The church is now seen to be on the outside of the cultural mainstream, and its values are under attack. Christians in the 80's recognized this shift and began to push back against this trend by entering the political arena with their organizations and moral agenda.

What has developed over time is a viewpoint among the unsaved, which thinks that the Christian religion is as much a political entity as it is religious. Because of this, its opponents resist Christianity in the same way you would resist a political party that is not the one of your choosing. The question we need to ask ourselves is what has happened to the message of Jesus and the proclamation of the Good News?

Government, secular humanism, and other religions have taken over to a greater degree the ministry to the poor and disenfranchised in our societies. They have done this and gained influence with each new generation as the church looks on while being distracted by other things. We simply did not recognize that this was to become a lost opportunity for the gospel.

It's time for a new generation of leaders to arise that carry the heart of Isaiah 58 and move in the power mantle of Isaiah 61. It is my prayer for you that kingdom strategies will be released to you that are tailored to the needs of the communities and cities in which you serve. I pray that those who take up this mandate and mantle will see a like-minded gathering of believers who come together to bring this ministry to its rightful place in the body of Christ.

To those ministries that are already dedicated to being blessings to the poor, I would offer this advice: You have made do with so little for so long that it is time to raise your expectations. You took on this ministry because of your love for people and your servant's heart, but it is time to begin to lay claim to all that Isaiah 58 promises for your ministry and your family.

In my years of contact with those that serve in these ministries, greed or want does not seem to be part of their DNA. Therefore, I feel as though I need to exhort you to prove the promise of God and begin to dream again, and dream big. It is very easy in this kind of environment to cede to the low expectation of the poverty spirit. After reading the 58th chapter, can you honestly say to yourself that God is not making extravagant promises of favor and blessings to you?

> *"Give, and it will be given to you. A good measure, pressed down, shaken together and running over, will be poured into your lap. For with the measure you use, it will be measured to you"* (Luke 6:38).

It is also time for you to add to your ministry, the expectation of a greater release in the gifts of healing and miracles. I serve as a director of a foundation in Switzerland that has for many years carried this heart and care for the poor. Andreas Kunz the chairman of Noiva Foundation has seen the combination of ministry and mandate in their operational teams who simply sought to be a blessing in the refugee camps and cities of the Islamic nations of the Middle East. In bringing food, clothing, and other basic necessities of life to Muslims from the war-torn regions, the door is open to pray with and for them with God providing the power demonstration of the Holy Spirit for healing and miracles.

Through these simple acts of kindness, the doors have opened in these nations for Noiva to initiate non-political forums for reconciliation between Israel and its Arab neighbors with government leaders of both people groups participating. Reconciliation between Arabs and Jews has now become a major focus of Noiva with growing acceptance to its vision of peace in Israel and some Middle Eastern nations. This was the Lord's doing and was marvelous to see; its genesis came from simply wanting to manifest the love of God to those in need.

I could go on and on relating stories where God is doing mighty exploits and dramatic moves of His Spirit. He uses dear saints that are moved out of a heart of love for the poor and the lost without any connection or foreknowledge of the promises given through Isaiah's word. I believe now is the time for leadership to take hold of this season of harvest and opportunity.

Jesus gave us a clue as to where the fields were most ready for harvest. In the parable of the great banquet as told from Luke 14, we read of a master of a great house who has prepared a banquet and sends out his servants with invitations to his guests. One after another declines the invitation because they are too busy with their own lives and have no interest in attending the banquet. The offended host then tells his servants to fill his banquet hall in the following way,

> 21 The servant came back and reported this to his master. Then the owner of the house became angry and ordered his servant, 'Go out quickly into the streets and alleys of the town and bring in the poor, the crippled, the blind and the lame.'
>
> 22"'Sir,' the servant said, 'what you ordered has been done, but there is still room.'
>
> 23"Then the master told his servant, 'Go out to the roads and country lanes and compel them to come in, so that my house will be full. 24I tell you, not one of those who were invited will get a taste of my banquet'" (Luke 14:21-24).

Is this not a clear direction for our evangelistic ministries to hone their strategies and lead us to reap in the ripe harvest field? The Lord makes some things so obvious to us, and it is like not seeing the forest because of the trees.

It is the vulnerability of our human condition that we want to be embraced by the A-listers of our society and not be found among the ranks of the lessor. Notice what James had to say in his epistle of the first century. His words only prove that little has changed in two thousand years:

> *Listen, my dear brothers and sisters: Has not God chosen those who are poor in the eyes of the world to be rich in faith and to inherit the kingdom he promised those who love him? 6But you have dishonored the poor. Is it not the rich who are exploiting you? Are they not the ones who are dragging you into court? 7Are they not the ones who are blaspheming the noble name of him to whom you belong?* (James 2:5-7).

Our populations amass among the lower ranks of society. If we win the hearts and minds for Jesus amongst these classes, we win our cities for God. I am reminded of a picture I had in my mind during an early morning time of prayer.

I saw a building that was square in its foundation being built vertically. As the vision zoomed in for a more detailed inspection, I could see that the stones of the building were like a crystal with living faces within these blocks. It reminded me of those decorative glass blocks that are used in home construction. I recognized some of the faces that made up these living stones. It was obvious to me then, that what I was seeing was a picture of the body of Christ in the city I was living in. In Peter's epistle he writes of this symbolic picture:

> *"As you come to him, the living Stone—rejected by humans but chosen by God and precious to him— 5you also, like living stones, are being built into a spiritual house to be a holy priesthood, offering spiritual sacrifices acceptable to God through Jesus Christ"* (1 Peter 2:4,5).

The scene in that vision then panned across the landscape to another fortress castle-like structure that had the appearance of dark black glass. As the scene zoomed in for closer inspection, I could see its black stones were of a similar glass block design and that it also had within it, living faces, some of whom I recognized. I knew I was looking at a spiritual principality ruling within my home city. I had never thought or considered that the enemy's stronghold could carry in its imagery, something similar to the picture of the church of God. Behind the walls of those living stones sat a power ruling in relative safety shielded from the arrows of intercession that were being volleyed against it. I knew that in order to dethrone that ruler, we would have to breach the wall. As the Good News of Jesus was proclaimed to this wall I would see one stone move out from its structure and be placed into the crystal wall of the kingdom of God. With every stone removed from the wall of the enemy, his fortress was weakened. I realized that any outpouring of the Spirit within the city could create a significant breach in the wall and transfer those stones out of the darkness and into the structure of light.

This changed my perspective of how spiritual warfare is to be conducted. If the spiritual leadership within our cities would focus its attention on the proclamation of the Good News in all of its forms of evangelism and bring the invitation to those communities that are in need, we will breach the spiritual walls that hold captive those citizens. We need to move from a fixed model of warfare like that of the Great War, where each side is entrenched and separated by a "no man's land" to a mobile and engaging warfare of the manifest love of God in word, power, and deed. We need to crossover and engage those who are held captive and set them free in Jesus' name!

It may be that your church of affluence would plant a church in the impoverished areas of your city or co-labor and support ministries that are already on the frontlines with laborers and financial commitment to those already faithful works. It may be that the various ministry gifts in your city can do regular outreaches of support out of those giftings and offer them as a part of the tactical support to those already established works. Everyone has something to offer; everyone has a role to serve in, let us work together and breach the wall no matter how great or how small. If we will do this, God will not allow Isaiah's prophetic word to fall to the ground. We will see the noonday sun of the glory of God shine upon us all.

Our Father, raise up the dread champions. Raise up Your vision and strategies from among Your people whoever they may be and stir up Your people to action. Let rivers of creativity flow and let these works be fully furnished with Your provision and supply. Awaken our hearts and minds to the new opportunities that this season affords us and mobilize Your people from all of Your various streams to work together in love. Use us to breach these walls and bring as an offering to the Lord Jesus, His reward in the form of many sons and daughters into the kingdom of God. Raise up a holy passion for Your glory, in Jesus' name, we pray. Amen

Epilogue

Closing Thoughts

Some of you may have thought in reading this book that you have been led down a road that you did not choose to go. You wanted a book that would show you the power of the fast in prayer and intercession. I must tell that I felt the same way when challenged by the Lord on this subject. But remember, it was God who declared the fast that He has chosen for His sons and daughters. It was God who showed us that His fast was about ministry and not at all about food.

So then, does fasting have any role in the life of a New Covenant believer? The answer to that is quite simple: it can have as large a role in your life as you choose for it to have. You are not under any constraint to fast or not to fast; it is always about the true intent of the heart.

The apostle Paul did not teach on fasting but he had a lot to say on matters concerning food in his letters. That in and of itself should say a lot to you as he tackled all the main issues for the early church, whether it was spiritual or societal. The big issue of their day was whether or not a Christian could eat meats that were sacrificed to idols. Another issue that Paul was contending with was the pressure by Jewish believers to make Gentile believers conform to the Law of Moses. This was not just about circumcision; it was about following Jewish holy days, which would have included fasting as we learned from the previous chapters. His contention with those that wanted to mix Judaism with the new faith could not be made more clear than in his letter to the Galatians. Here are a few things that Paul had to say on matters concerning food from his other letters.

> 1Accept the one whose faith is weak, without quarreling over disputable matters. 2One person's faith allows them to eat anything, but another, whose faith is weak, eats only vegetables. 3The one who eats everything must not treat with contempt the one who does not, and the one who does not eat everything must not judge the one who does, for God has accepted them. 4Who are you to judge someone else's servant? To their own master, servants stand or fall. And they will stand, for the Lord is able to make them stand.
>
> 5One person considers one day more sacred than another; another considers every day alike. Each of them should be fully convinced in their own mind. 6Whoever regards one day as special does so to the Lord. Whoever eats meat does so to the Lord, for they give thanks to God; and whoever abstains does so to the Lord and gives thanks to God. 7For none of us lives for ourselves alone, and none of us dies for ourselves alone. 8If we live, we live for the Lord; and if we die, we die for the Lord. So, whether we live or die, we belong to the Lord. 9For this very reason, Christ died and returned to life so that he might be the Lord of both the dead and the living (Romans 14:1-9).

> *"For the kingdom of God is not a matter of eating and drinking, but of righteousness, peace and joy in the Holy Spirit, 18because anyone who serves Christ in this way is pleasing to God and receives human approval"* (Romans 14:17,18).
>
> *"Therefore do not let anyone judge you by what you eat or drink, or with regard to a religious festival, a New Moon celebration or a Sabbath day. 17These are a shadow of the things that were to come; the reality, however, is found in Christ"* (Colossians 2:16, 17).
>
> *20Since you died with Christ to the elemental spiritual forces of this world, why, as though you still belonged to the world, do you submit to its rules: 21"Do not handle! Do not taste! Do not touch!"? 22These rules, which have to do with things that are all destined to perish with use, are based on merely human commands and teachings. 23Such regulations indeed have an appearance of wisdom, with their self-imposed worship, their false humility and their harsh treatment of the body, but they lack any value in restraining sensual indulgence* (Colossians 2:20-23).

My hope is that this book has provoked your thinking while at the same time has awakened a desire in you to walk in the Isaiah 58 mantle and continue the ministry of the Isaiah 61 mandate of the Lord Jesus. Let us co-labor in His work and be a part of expanding His inheritance in the earth, one person at a time or with a move of God that brings in the lost by the thousands.

You are blessed! Now, be the blessing and break the fast of the hungry.

About the Author

T M Leszko has spent over 30 years in combined ministry and the corporate world. His current business interests are on three continents but his focus is shifting to writing and ministry.

He also serves as a director of the Noiva Foundation. The organization's chief purpose is to work towards a non-political solution for reconciliation between Israel and its neighboring Arab nations. In working with governments and the private sector, Noiva has found a willingness in those from both sides of the political and cultural spectrum to work towards peace in the Middle East.

Noiva also shares a vibrant vision of ministry that provides aid to the poor in the Middle East and Africa. For more information please visit our website at *www.noiva.ch*

www.ingramcontent.com/pod-product-compliance
Lightning Source LLC
Chambersburg PA
CBHW070619300426
44113CB00010B/1590